2 BECOMING ONE™
WORKBOOK

God Created
MARRIAGE
He Can Make it Work

DON & SALLY MEREDITH

Christian FamilyLife
Charlotte, North Carolina

Christian Family Life, Inc.
5301 W.T. Harris Boulevard • Charlotte, NC 28269
Phone: (704) 596-9630 • Fax: (704) 596-4255

ISBN 0-9657965-3-1

1 3 5 7 9 10 8 6 4 2

Printed in the United States of America

A Publication of Christian Family Life, Inc.

Christian Family Life teaches engaged and married couples God's faith principles for marriage
so they may know Christ more intimately and be free to serve Him more effectively.
The ministry of Christian Family Life is extended primarily through small groups,
publications, Sunday School, and the Internet. For more information about Christian Family Life,
please visit us on the Internet at www.2becoming1.com.

To order resources please go to www.2becoming1.com, or call toll-free (800) 264-3876.

BECOMING 2 ONE™

Table of
CONTENTS

Introduction: Starting the Journey Toward Oneness 5

PART ONE: GOD'S PART
Accepting by Faith God's Principles for Oneness

Week One: Our Roadblock and God's Purposes for Marriage 11

Week Two: God's Provision for Oneness 27

Week Three: God's Power for Oneness: The Ministry of the Holy Spirit 43

Week Four: God's Instruments for Change: Love and Blessing 63

Week Five: God's Order for Marital Oneness: Mutual Love and Respect. 85

PART TWO: OUR PART
Acting by Faith on God's Principles for Oneness

Week Six: Marital Trials. 105

Week Seven: Romance and Sexual Fulfillment 123

Week Eight: Communication and Resolving Conflict 143

Conclusion: Continuing the Journey. 162

Appendices: Prayer Journals, Recommitment of Marriage Vows,
Memory Verse Cards. 167

Starting the
JOURNEY
toward Oneness

*...the **two** will **become one** flesh.*

<small>MATTHEW 19:5</small>

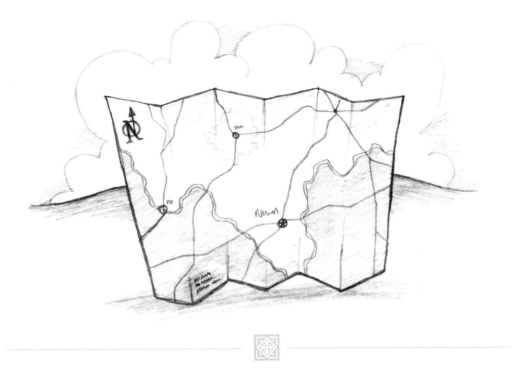

PURPOSE OF THE JOURNEY

Ever wonder where God put the operating manual for marriage? If He designed marriage, can He make it work?

The wedding day is both a celebration and a launch. You celebrate your consecration before God, and you embark on a new journey as man and wife. You go from saying, "I do," to "Now what?" It doesn't take long for many couples to find their marriage bogged down on the rugged terrain of conflict, complacency, and self-centeredness, never reaching the summit of true intimacy.

Where is your marriage heading? Intimacy or irritation?

What stalls most couples in their journey towards intimacy is their preoccupation with *performance*. We see our spouse as the problem rather than God's provision for our needs. We blame more than bless. We move from an infatuation over our spouse's strengths to a fixation on their weaknesses. In short, we expect them to perform to our liking before we move towards intimacy.

God said in the Garden, "For this reason a man shall leave his father and his mother and be joined to his wife and they shall become one flesh" (Gen. 2:24). Marriage, from God's perspective, is simply "becoming one." That's what marriage is all about, pursuing "oneness." The goal of this study is to help you "become one" by searching God's Word for guidance on building a Christ-centered marriage.

When confronted with relationship issues in marriage, your natural first response will be to expect your spouse to change and fix the problem. But that path only leads to dead-ends in marriage. If true intimacy is your goal in marriage, it will mean depending on something outside your own strength – namely faith in God and His manual for marriage, Scripture.

In this study, your marriage will embark on a journey from a *performance-based relationship* to a *faith-based relationship*. Along the way, you will be exhorted to:

- **Accept** by faith God's principles for oneness.
- **Act** by faith on God's principles for oneness.

As we begin *Two Becoming One*, there are four things we must keep in mind.

1. We were created for relationships.

First, God created us for relationships, both with Himself and with others. It was Saint Augustine who said, "You have created us for Yourself, O God, and our hearts are restless until they find their rest in You." The whole Scripture speaks of our relationship with Him: how to have it, how to hold onto it, how to rest in it, how to communicate it, how to enjoy it.

But, God did not want us to just have relationship with Him alone. He created others that we might also learn to live with and love those He places in our lives. Love and relationships are a central theme in the Bible, beginning in Genesis and culminating in Revelation. If relationships are so incredibly important to God, we must ask ourselves the question: Why marriage? What is it about marriage that is so important to God? What is it about marriage that is so important to us?

2. We are to be conformed to the image of Jesus Christ.

Could it be that God created marriage, the most intimate of human relationships, as one of His primary purposes for refining us, for chiseling off our selfish human nature, and for making us more "other-centered"? Is this what He means when He says that we are being conformed to the image of Jesus Christ (Romans 8:29 – "For whom He foreknew, He also predestined to become conformed to the image of His Son …")? How best to make us "other-centered" than to give us a spouse, very different from us, to hone us into His image? And this process takes time, in fact, a whole lifetime. It takes study. It takes work. It takes, if you will, blood, sweat,

and tears. Is that why marriage is to be life-long—"till death do us part"?

The goal of this study is not to build a great marriage. It's to build a great marriage that glorifies and serves God. Marriage is not God's primary focus and purpose. Our greatest goal in life and marriage should be loving and serving God (see Mark 12:30; Matthew 28:19–20). Through marriage God shapes us into the image of His Son, so we might train our children and help change the world through His grace.

3. Marriage is a covenant.

God created marriage as a covenant (Proverbs 2:16-17; Malachi 2:14-16). In the eyes of God, a marital covenant is a legally binding contract that is to be ratified or confirmed publicly before God Himself and His witnesses (i.e., the believing community). Biblically-based marriage vows not only express our divinely-ordained commitment to each other, but they also seal our marital covenant before God, binding us to Him, to each other, and to His people—for the rest of our lives! For God said, "What God has brought together, let no man separate" (Matthew 19:6).

4. Marriage is a commitment.

God's covenant of marriage is sustained and ultimately fulfilled through our commitment, first to Him and then to our spouse. Through marriage, we voluntarily give up ourselves to please the heart of another, first God and then our spouse. Through marriage, we not only take on one other person (our spouse) but others (our children) whom we will train in the very lessons that we are learning.

By the end of our eight weeks, we trust you will be well on your way towards the goal God has for every marriage … oneness.

STRUCTURE OF THE JOURNEY

Each chapter in our journey will be composed of the following sections. Below, you will find a brief description of what to expect as you embark on your study each week:

A Quick Look Ahead - Before you leave for any journey, it's a good idea to figure out where you are going. At the beginning of each chapter, you'll see exactly where you are heading in the coming week.

2B1 Companion Book – Throughout the chapters you will be asked to consult the companion book for this study, *Two Becoming One*, by Don and Sally Meredith.

Memory Verse – The Psalmist says, "Your Word I have treasured in my heart, that I may not sin against You" (Ps. 119:11). Moving from *performance* to *faith* in our marriages will require guiding wisdom from God. Each week you and your spouse will be asked to memorize a Scripture that, if applied, can help you achieve oneness.

Faith Steps – Knowledge will be useless without application. To help you move from *performance* to *faith*, these sections will apply the lessons learned the week before. These are personal and will not be shared in class.

Daily Walk – For five out of the seven days in a week, each reader will answer questions and take a journey through material that will help them move from performance to faith.

Faith Principles – For the first five chapters, there will be a faith principle for oneness. Based on God's Word, these principles build a solid foundation for intimacy. The first part of this study will focus on understanding and accepting these principles. The second will be to act on them as we face some struggles of marriage. (In the last three chapters these are the **Personal Applications**.)

A Quick Look Back – At the end of each chapter, you will be able to survey the key concepts on your journey to oneness.

2B1 Prayer – To help you commit your study to the Lord, a prayer is offered at the end that you can pray with your spouse.

Thoughts for the Road – After you finish the *Daily Journeys* and the small group discussion, study notes are provided to go into greater detail about the principles learned that week.

The power of this study comes with your commitment to God and His Word, to your spouse and to those in your small group. To help with these commitments, you will find Scripture memory verses, a weekly prayer request form, and a suggested "recommitment" vow in the back of this manual.

GUIDELINES FOR THE JOURNEY

To make your small group effective, please consider these four practical guidelines:

1. Size

We believe your time will be most rewarding with somewhere between four to six couples.

2. Time and Place

The actual meeting time should take no more than two hours, but be sure to include time for prayer and fellowship. It's best to meet each week (eight weeks straight) for continuity. Whether you meet in homes or a church, make sure the place is comfortable and conducive for open and intimate conversation.

3. Atmosphere

Love and accountability are the key concepts that make the *Two Becoming One* small group experience successful. At no point should people feel pressured to share something too personal. However, mutual trust will help build mutual transparency that will enhance the small group discussion.

4. Commitments

In the first meeting your group will benefit by agreeing to commit to the following:

To your marriage – This study is for couples who desire a sincere pursuit of intimacy and depth. Each week you will be asked to complete in-depth questions and exercises. It is designed for couples who are in all stages of marriage – from engaged couples to those with grandchildren. *However, couples who are struggling with serious marital, emotional, sexual, or spiritual issues may need to consult a professional counselor before taking this study.*

To the daily journeys, faith steps, reading, and Scripture memory – Your reward for finishing this journey will be determined in large part by how much you engage with the homework, applications, reading, and your spiritual walk with God. The reading, homework, and personal application should only take you about one or two hours a week. Finishing the homework each week is crucial to the overall atmosphere of the discussion group. **Each spouse needs his or her own individual workbook.**

To the group – It's hard to build trust and openness with couples unless you commit your time and energy. View these weeks as a priority – even sacred – and necessary to your pursuit of oneness as a couple. Prayerfully commit with your spouse to attend, and be ready to participate in most of the meetings.

To the leader – Please reference the *Two Becoming One* leader's guide to ensure that complete answers are given. Also, to help you in your preparation, please listen to the leader's audio CD each week. The leader's guide and CD can be ordered at www.2becoming1.com.

Social

This study is designed to create strong relationships among the couples in each small group. Because of this, we highly recommend that each group plan a social time together once the study has been completed. Many groups have used this social time as an opportunity to share, to fellowship, even to strategize on how to help other marriages in their churches become faith based.

Let's begin the journey to oneness!

ONENESS...God's Part

Accepting by Faith:

God's Purposes for Marriage
(Week One)

God's Provision for Oneness
(Week Two)

God's Power for Oneness
(Week Three)

God's Instruments for Change
(Week Four)

God's Order for Marital Oneness
(Week Five)

WEEK ONE:

Our Roadblock and
GOD'S PURPOSES
for Marriage

God created man in His own image,

in the image of God He created him;

male and female He created them

(GENESIS 1:27).

OUR ROADBLOCK AND GOD'S PURPOSES FOR ONENESS

Four words said it all. They appeared printed in bold type inside the store window of a Hollywood jewelry store. "WE RENT WEDDING RINGS." Hollywood weddings highlight all the grocery store magazines. When was the last time you saw a 50th anniversary on the same covers? For many, marriage has turned into a one-day event rather than a lifelong commitment.

Anyone can get married; few can sustain a marriage.

What stands between you and divorce? How about this question: What road-blocks keep you from true intimacy in your marriage? If 33% of all marriages, both Christian and non-Christian, end in divorce or separation, what's the percentage of marriages that end in intimacy? Many who marry their "soul mate" end up three years later with a "roommate."

Where are you today? Nearlywed? Newlywed? Scratching the seven-year itch or celebrating thirty years of marital commitment? Regardless of your stage in marriage, enraptured or nearing rupture, if you have picked up this workbook, it's a safe bet you desire what God created in the heart of every man and woman: a desire for intimacy, for transparency, for oneness.

A QUICK LOOK AHEAD

Why do marriages fail? Think about it for a minute. A wedding day is filled with good intentions and heartfelt promises. How do we go from saying "I do" to "Get out!"? In this lesson we will explore the primary reason most marriages experience a roadblock to oneness: They fail to move from a performance-based relationship to a faith-based relationship.

To move beyond this roadblock, we must be willing to accept God's five faith principles for oneness. In this first week, not only will we examine some road blocks to true marital intimacy, we will discover the first faith principle for oneness.

Ask yourself this question, "What is the purpose of my marriage?"
- So I won't be lonely?
- To have children?
- Because I fell in love?

You may be surprised to discover that the Author of marriage has three clear purposes for marriage that will start us on our journey from performance to faith. In our study of Genesis 1, we will discover how those three purposes will encompass our first faith-principle for oneness.

Before you begin your first daily journey, read chapters 1-3 in your companion book, Two Becoming One, *by Don and Sally Meredith.*

1 DAILY WALK, DAY ONE

1. From the companion book, *Two Becoming One*, chapter two, list the six reasons why marriages fail.

_____

_____

_____

_____

_____

2. In light of these six reasons, the biggest struggle facing my marriage is
_____ because:

_____

_____

_____

3. As you look at the four stages of marital decline found in chapter three of *Two Becoming One,* list the four stages and then state which stage most accurately describes your marriage relationship and why?

Days

_____

_____

_____

_____

_____

4. Most couples operate on the belief that each spouse needs to "do their share." Looking at the chart below, describe a situation in your marriage where you went through this cycle:

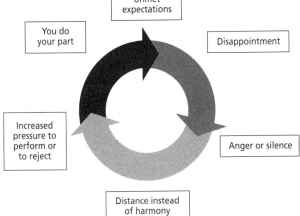

Figure 1
The Cycle of Unmet Expectations

_____

_____

_____

_____

_____

_____

_____

_____

_____

Most couples define love in terms of how they feel. There can be no weaker foundation for a relationship.

2 DAILY WALK, DAY TWO

1. Read 1 Peter 2:21-25 below:

For you have been called for this purpose, since Christ also suffered for you, leaving you an example for you to follow in His steps, who committed no sin, nor was any deceit found in his mouth; and while being reviled, He did not revile in return; while suffering, He uttered no threats, but kept entrusting Himself to him who judges righteously; and He Himself bore our sins in His body on the cross, so that we might die to sin and live to righteousness; for by His wounds you were healed. For you were continually straying like sheep, but now you have returned to the Shepherd and Guardian of your souls.

How did Christ respond to those who "reviled" him?

_____

_____

_____

2. How did you respond the last time your spouse hurt you?

_____

_____

_____

After writing down your experience, if you responded negatively, seek forgiveness from God (1 John 1:9), then go to your spouse. In explaining how you were hurt, hopefully your spouse will in turn seek forgiveness for his or her infraction, but don't expect it! That would be moving back from a *faith-based relationship* to a *performance-based relationship*.

3. Look up John 17:20-21. What does "oneness" mean here, and how can that be applied to marriage?

_____

_____

_____

_____

Before you begin the next daily journey, read chapter four in your companion book, Two Becoming One, *by Don and Sally Meredith.*

3 DAILY WALK, DAY THREE

In the first chapter of Genesis, we read that God created the earth. From His description of the creation of mankind in verses 26 to 31, we can observe three purposes He has for mankind. Let's look at the first one found in Genesis 1:26-27 below:

Then God said, 'Let us make man in our image, in our likeness.' ... So God created man in his own image, in the image of God he created him, male and female he created them (GENESIS 1:26–27).

1. What is God's first purpose for your marriage? What is meant by "image"?

_____

_____

_____

2. Although each human being is created uniquely in God's image, married couples have a unique opportunity to reflect the divine image as a couple. Why is this important?

_____

_____

_____

3. How does God use marriage to conform us to the image of Jesus Christ? Look up Romans 8:28-30. (See pg. 6, #2)

_____

_____

[4] DAILY WALK, DAY FOUR

God's second purpose is found in Genesis 1:28a: "God blessed them and said to them, 'Be fruitful and increase in number; fill the earth'" (see also Malachi 2:15).

1. What is God's second purpose for your marriage?

_____

_____

2. What do "blessed" and "be fruitful" mean in light of God's second purpose?

_____

_____

3. God clearly wants parents to do more than just raise children. If you are a parent, He wants you and your spouse to reproduce God's image in your children. From the following verses, list as many specific instructions as you can concerning raising godly children.

Psalm 127:1, 3–5

_____

_____

Deuteronomy 6:4–7

_____

_____

Prov. 22:6

_____

_____

4. God does not limit reproducing His image just to child rearing. Read Matthew 28:18–20. What are all Christians called to do?

_____

_____

5️⃣ Daily Walk, Day Five

God's third purpose for marriage is found in Genesis 1:28: "And God blessed them; and said to them, 'Subdue [the earth]. Rule over the fish of the sea and the birds of the air and over every living creature that moves on the ground.'"

1   Based on the above command to Adam and Eve, what do you think is God's third purpose for your marriage?

_____

_____

_____

_____

2.   What does the plural pronoun "them" tell us about the relationship and responsibilities of Adam and Eve in fulfilling this third purpose?

_____

_____

_____

_____

3. Read Ephesians 6:10-12 below:

Finally, be strong in the Lord and in the strength of His might. Put on the full armor of God, so that you will be able to stand firm against the schemes of the devil. For our struggle is not against flesh and blood, but against the rulers, against the powers, against the worldly forces of this darkness, against the spiritual forces of wickedness in the heavenly places (emphasis added).

God gave men and women the responsibility to reign over the physical earth. In addition, after the Fall (Genesis 3), God instructed us to reign in spiritual warfare. Who is our struggle against?

_____

4. Satan attempted to destroy the oneness of the Father and the Son. He also attempts to destroy oneness in your marriage (read John 10:10). List several ways that Satan has attacked your marriage and family.

_____

_____

_____

So God's **FIRST** Faith-Based Principle for Oneness is This:

By faith, we must commit ourselves to God's purposes of reflecting His image, reproducing a godly heritage, and reigning in spiritual warfare.

☞ *Apply the Principle* ☜

1. The three purposes for marriage can be expressed with three "R's" shown below. How could your marriage improve in each area?

Reflecting God's image –

_____

_____

_____

Reproducing a godly heritage –

_____

_____

_____

Reigning in spiritual warfare –

_____

_____

_____

2. List several ways each of the following has hindered your ability to accomplish God's purpose for your marriage:

Personal weakness –

_____

_____

_____

Family background –

_____

_____

_____

Lack of biblical knowledge of marriage –

_____

_____

_____

Satan –

_____

_____

_____

A QUICK LOOK BACK

Our roadblock to intimacy is our *performance-based view of marriage*. We see our spouse as the problem rather than focusing on God's solution for oneness. If we desire oneness with our spouse, we must, *by faith, commit ourselves to God's purposes of reflecting His image, reproducing a godly heritage, and reigning in spiritual warfare.*

 BECOMING ONE PRAYER

Heavenly Father, forgive me for viewing my spouse as the roadblock to oneness. My selfish desire to demand a certain level of performance has made me miss the blessing my spouse is and the purposes You have for my marriage. I commit to join with my spouse in oneness so that we might reflect Your image, reproduce godly children and disciples, and reign in spiritual warfare. Give each of us a desire to please and serve You in this way. Bless our marriage, home, and family. In the name of Jesus, Amen.

Complete the week one *Daily Walks* and small group discussion before reading these notes.

OUR ROADBLOCK TO ONENESS — A PERFORMANCE-BASED RELATIONSHIP

At the beginning of our chapter we discussed how anyone can get married, but few can sustain a marriage. Everyone hopes for a lifetime of intimacy on his or her wedding day, but many find themselves careening into a roadblock soon after the honeymoon.

Each spouse develops a natural, human plan for marital happiness. The couple's separate plans are based on the unique personalities and personal differences of each partner, including different family influences, role models, books, and often different church experiences. Because their plans for marital happiness are different, conflict usually results.

Most human plans have a similar flaw: *a focus on the spouse's performance.* Each believes, "I'll be happy when my spouse does what I want him or her to do." When one spouse focuses on the other's performance, it often leads to the destruction of the relationship.

All natural, human relationships start with the subtle motivation of attraction based on beauty, sex appeal, personality, wealth, power, intelligence, popularity, or any other source of human attraction. The long-term survival of the relationship is directly related to the ability to sustain these attractions. Each spouse must continue to perform at the original attraction level, or disappointment will result.

> Most human plans have a similar flaw: a focus on the spouse's performance.

Relying on your spouse's performance to maintain the original attraction does not work over the long term. Because each of us is self-centered, we constantly want to know what our spouse has done for us lately. Sadly, as time passes, we subconsciously revert to the "greener pasture syndrome" where we begin to compare our spouse's performance with our own pre-conceived ideas and expectations, making satisfaction with our spouse more and more elusive.

Following are the six primary factors that destroy marriages. They are commonly found in natural, human relationships:

1. Couples fail to anticipate differences resulting from diverse cultural backgrounds, differing family experiences, gender, and so on.

2. Couples buy into the notion of a "fifty-fifty" relationship, meaning they honestly expect their spouse to meet them halfway.

3. Society has taught us that mankind is basically good. Therefore, most husbands and wives fail to anticipate their selfish and self-centered natures.

4. Couples fail to cope with life's trials. When painful trials come into the marriage, instead of standing together through them, couples tend to blame each other or think something is wrong with one spouse or the other.

5. Many people have a fantasy view of love. We quickly feel stuck with an unloving person and become deceived into believing that the next one will be better.

6. Many people lack a vital relationship with Jesus Christ. It could be that they have never come to a specific point in time when they trusted in Christ as Savior and Lord by inviting them into their lives. Therefore, He has no impact on the marriage relationship.

GOD'S SOLUTION TO ONENESS — THE FAITH-BASED RELATIONSHIP

The faith relationship is opposite of the performance relationship in two significant ways. First, it is not natural at all—it is supernatural. You will only learn about this kind of relationship from God through His Word. Second, the faith relationship does not focus on the human performance of one's spouse but on God's character, promises, and faithfulness. The very Author and Perfector of our faith (Heb. 12:2) is also the Author and Perfector of our marriage.

This kind of relationship involves God as the Guarantor of the marriage with the specifics of the guarantee found in Scripture. God wants us to have a Christ-centered marriage relationship and offers us a blessing when we "live in harmony with one another" and are "compassionate and humble." We are to heed this divine calling, Peter wrote, so that we "may inherit a blessing" (1 Peter 3:8–9).

The key difference of the faith relationship is its long-term hope based on God's character and faithfulness. We know He is good and He cares about what happens to us. He loves us. God's guidance for us to marry a certain person becomes more important than human attraction. The more mature we are spiritually, the more God will be able to solidify our calling to each other through Scripture and wise counsel. We understand that God has directed us to love each other for life. This ability to follow God's leading takes over when human attractions and performance fail.

A question that commonly comes up when discussing faith relationships is, "Can God fulfill my needs in this relationship in spite of my spouse's weaknesses?" The answer is yes! If God can meet your needs anyway, then your spouse's weaknesses no longer limit you. This fact frees husbands and wives to love one another unconditionally as they thank God for His gracious provision.

By trusting in the example of Christ in 1 Peter 2:21-25, and by believing

> The key difference of the faith relationship is its long-term hope based on God's character and faithfulness.

and acting on God's Word, faith allows us to override our natural human instinct to change each other. "Faith is being sure of what we hope for ..." (Hebrews 11:1, see also verse 6); such faith pleases God as well.

1 Peter 2:23 states, "but (Jesus) kept entrusting Himself to Him who judges righteously." This statement confirms Christ's faith in His Father. Jesus believed in God's sovereign plan more than His desire to abandon the cross, more than His disappointment over Peter's denials, and more than His desire for His persecutors to receive instant justice. *He based His relationships on faith in God rather than on the performance of man.* Spouses who base his or her marriage on performance will naturally reward unmet expectations with anger or silence, lashing out when hurt, or believing justice for any infraction must be executed immediately.

Christians can choose a faith relationship, founded on their faith in Jesus Christ. In Matthew 19:4-6, Jesus Himself called couples to oneness in marriage, quoting Genesis 2:24, and concluded, "So they are no longer two, but one."

	RELATIONSHIPS: NATURAL/HUMAN VS. SUPERNATURAL/FAITH		
	Natural/Human Relationship		Supernatural/Faith Relationship
Basic motivation	Appearance Popularity Finances Sex appeal	Politics Personality Intellect Escape	Circumstances and human attraction are only initially important. Both parties are ultimately directed by God through His Word, confirmed by wise counsel.
Basis of Success	Continual human performance		God's faithfulness through His promises
Long-term Results	Rejection Hurt Conflict Resentment	Disappointment Lost feelings Lost commitment Lost oneness	Faith Blessing Love Hope Oneness Lasting commitment Compassion

OUR NEED FOR ONENESS

"*Spiritual oneness*" *in relationships can be defined as being in agreement with God and His purposes and with one another.* When we are not one in marriage, we block a major avenue through which God meets our desperate need for love.

The Bible reveals God's desire for oneness between mankind and Himself. On the night before His death, Christ prayed for unity, "that all of them may be one, Father, just as you are in Me and I am in You" (see John 17:20–21).

We also see that God desires oneness between ourselves and other people. He confirmed this when He established oneness as the hope of marriage in Genesis 2:24: "For this reason a man will leave his father and mother and be united to his wife, and they will become one flesh." This need for oneness extends to relationships among Christians, who are referred to as the body of Christ (see Romans 12:4–5).

GOD'S PATH TO ONENESS

Scripture offers a path to help us accomplish the goal of marital oneness:

Then God said, "Let us make man in Our image, in Our likeness, and let them rule over the fish of the sea and the birds of the air, over the livestock, over all the earth, and over all the creatures that move along the ground. So God created man in His own image, in the image of God He created him; male and female He created them. God blessed them and said to them, "Be fruitful and increase in number; fill the earth and subdue it. Rule over the fish of the sea and the birds of the air and over every living creature that moves on the ground" (Gen 1:26-28).

In effect, we are beginning to move from performance to faith in our marriages. In this workbook, we will study a simple, two-part method to achieving oneness in your marriage:

1. Accept by faith God's principles for oneness

2. Act in faith on God's principles for oneness.

GOD'S PURPOSES FOR ONENESS

*O*ur first faith principle is: *By faith, we must commit ourselves to God's purposes of reflecting His image, reproducing a godly heritage, and reigning in spiritual warfare.* God had three distinct purposes for creating human life in general and marriage in particular.

1. Purpose one: Reflect the image of God through oneness (Genesis 1:26–27).

Note the phrases "in our image" and "in our likeness." God is clearly stating that He made Adam and Eve to be a reflection of Himself. While both Adam and Eve reflected God's image individually, in Genesis 1:27 God gave them the unique opportunity as husband and wife to reflect their Creator through oneness: "in the image of God he created him [Adam], male and female he created them." In the New Testament (Romans 8:29), we see that

God is in the process of conforming us into the "image" of Jesus Christ. He uses our marriages for this purpose (Ephesians 5:22-33). We are to be reflectors of God's light to a darkened world (Matt. 5:14).

2. Purpose two: Reproduce a godly heritage through oneness (Genesis 1:28a).

If you put this verse in the context of the rest of Scripture, it is clear that simply having children is not the full purpose that God intended here (see Deuteronomy 6:1–9; Psalm 127:1, 3–5; Proverbs 22:6). This purpose could better be stated as "to reproduce a godly heritage that will also reflect God." This would include the reproducing of "spiritual children" or disciples. God Himself adopted us as His own children forever when we trusted Christ as our personal Savior (Romans 8:15, 23; Galatians 4:4–6;

Ephesians 1:5–6). In addition, all believers are called to reproduce God's image in spiritual children (disciples – Matt. 28:19).

3. Purpose three: Reign in spiritual warfare through oneness (Genesis 1:28b).

Through oneness in marriage, husbands and wives are equipped to exercise dominion and rule over God's physical creation of planet Earth.

God also intended husbands and wives to thwart Satan as they rule the earth spiritually through oneness with God and each other (Hebrews 2:6–8; Ephesians 6:10–13; John 8:43–45). Even though individually they are weaker in creation than Satan and his forces, a couple can overcome Satan's schemes by depending on God together.

GOD'S PURPOSES FOR ONENESS REQUIRE COMMITMENT.

God's intention for marriage is clear. Every marriage is a part of His plan. Are you aware that your marriage is vital to God today? Consider making these three commitments as a response to God's purposes for your marriage:

1. Agree with God's purposes of reflecting, reproducing, and reigning.

2. Ask forgiveness of God and your spouse for not following God's purposes in the past.

3. Make a commitment to God and to your spouse to follow God's purposes from this day forth.

God is unchanging (see Heb. 13:8). Therefore, His plan for marriage is unaltered. We are either going to believe Him or we are not. Either we will follow His purposes and experience marital unity and harmony, or we will not fully experience the blessing He intends in marriage. It is our choice.

Regardless of whether you are nearly-wed, newlywed, or celebrating thirty years of marriage, ask yourself how you can focus on God's purposes for marriage: reflect, reproduce, and reign.

> Are you aware that your marriage is vital to God today?

WEEK TWO:

God's

PROVISION

for Oneness

For this cause a man shall leave his

father and his mother,

and shall cleave to his wife;

and they shall become one flesh

(Genesis 2:24, NASB).

God's Provision for Oneness

A wedding is one thing; a marriage is another. You remember your wedding day don't you? Soft music, rows of candles, flowing dresses, regal tuxedos, close friends and family members all framed by flowers in eternal bloom. Unfortunately, the beauty of the wedding day can, and often does, wilt under the pressure of expectations, miscommunication, and *performance*. Matrimonial bliss has the potential to turn into marital blunders.

Many people today talk about finding their "soul mate," someone who can satisfy their deepest longings. Unfortunately it doesn't take long for newlyweds to discover that no one person has everything. Each of us has weaknesses.

Our infatuation with our spouse's strengths before the wedding day is usually replaced with a fixation on our spouse's weaknesses after the wedding day. Wives soon realize their knight in shining armor was wearing aluminum. Husbands wonder how the tiara slipped off their princess bride. Once our focus turns to our spouse's deficiencies we begin to miss God's provision for our deepest intimacy needs.

A QUICK LOOK AHEAD

There are many chapters in Scripture that stand out for their teaching. If you want to talk salvation, you'll turn to John 3. If you want to review the Ten Commandments, you'll flip to Exodus 20. Love? 1Corinthians 13. Faith? Hebrews 11. What about marriage? Certainly Ephesians 5 and 1 Peter 3 are key, but any practical discussion on marriage will need to start in the very beginning... Genesis 2.

Last week we began our journey from a *performance-based relationship* to a *faith-based relationship* by accepting God's three purposes for oneness. This week we will take the next step... accepting by faith God's provision for oneness.

Ask yourself this question, "How does God meet my deepest needs?"

- Through work?
- Through family?
- Through church?

In our study of Genesis 2, the Magna Carta of Marriage, we will discover what God's provision is for our deep need of intimacy.

 DAILY WALK, DAY ONE

Make sure you read last week's study notes before starting this section.
Review:

1. From your reading of last week's study notes, how would you describe the difference between a *performance-based relationship* and a *faith-based relationship*?

_____

_____

_____

_____

2. List and explain God's three purposes for marriage:

_____

_____

_____

_____

3. Which of the three purposes do you and your spouse struggle with the most and why?

_____

_____

✦ Faith Steps ✦

Remember, these exercises will not be discussed in class.

Part One (Personal)

In response to each of the statements in the chart below, draw a circle around the number that best describes your success as a couple. Use the following scale:

1= never, 2= rarely, 3= sometimes, 4= often, and 5= always

Then repeat the exercise, drawing an "X" through the number that best describes the way you think your spouse would appraise your success as a couple.

———— FULFILLING GOD'S PURPOSES IN OUR MARRIAGE ————

My mate and I experience oneness and endearment in our relationship	1	2	3	4	5
My mate and I reflect a godly image in our home and lives.	1	2	3	4	5
My mate and I reproduce a godly heritage through children and disciples of Jesus Christ.	1	2	3	4	5
My mate and I reign (rule) in spiritual warfare.	1	2	3	4	5

Part Two (Personal and as a Couple)

Spend some time alone with God and respond to the statements below. The purpose of this part of the application is to stimulate your commitment to God concerning His purposes for your life and marriage. Place a check mark in each box as you complete each step.

☐ Confess to God any past failure to reflect His image, reproduce a godly heritage, and reign in spiritual warfare.

☐ Commit to God to reflect, reproduce, and reign through oneness in the future.

☐ Share your new commitments with your spouse before the next *Two Becoming One* small group meeting. This can be done on the way to your small group.

2 DAILY WALK, DAY TWO

In Genesis 2:18-25, God moves from the big picture of creation discussed in Genesis 1:26-31, to the specific creation of man and woman. Through their story, God tells us how oneness in marriage is possible and reveals a four-step plan for achieving intimacy with your spouse that we will examine in the next four days.

1.   Read Genesis 2:18 below:

Then the Lord God said, "It is not good for the man to be alone; I will make him a helper suitable for him."

God was present with Adam in the Garden, yet He made a point of stating that Adam was alone. Why is this significant?

_____

_____

_____

_____

2.   Why is it important that you acknowledge that you have a God-created need for your spouse?

_____

_____

_____

_____

STEP ONE OF ACHIEVING INTIMACY:
God creates a need for companionship in our lives.

3 DAILY WALK, DAY THREE

1.   Read Genesis 2:19-20 below:

Out of the ground the Lord God formed every beast of the field and every bird of the sky, and brought them to the man to see what he would call them; and whatever the man called a living creature, that was its name. The man gave names to all the cattle, and to the birds of the sky, and to every beast of the field, but for Adam there was not found a helper suitable for him.

Before you begin your second daily journey, read chapter five in your companion book, Two Becoming One, *by Don and Sally Meredith.*

Thus, from the beginning of human history, relationships are not an option.

Why do you think God gave Adam the project of naming the animals?

_____

_____

_____

2. How do you think Adam discovered his need for intimacy?

_____

_____

_____

STEP TWO OF ACHIEVING INTIMACY:
God shows us our need for companionship.

4 DAILY WALK, DAY FOUR

1. Read Genesis 2:21-22 below:

    *So the Lord God caused a deep sleep to fall upon the man, and he slept;
    then He took one of his ribs and closed up the flesh at that place. The Lord
    God fashioned into a woman the rib which He had taken from the man,
    and brought her to the man.*

People today seem obsessed with finding someone to meet their needs, bouncing
from one relationship to another, always seeking satisfaction. How does this strategy
for finding the right spouse compare to the method God used with Adam?

_____

_____

_____

2. God, who created Eve, could have just placed her next to Adam before the
man awoke. Instead, God "brought her to the man." What does God's method of
involvement here teach us?

_____

_____

_____

Eve was not taken from his head to rule over him, nor from his feet to be beneath him, but was formed alongside him to complete him, and vice versa.

3. In what ways has God shown you your need for your spouse? Be specific.

_____

_____

_____

STEP THREE OF ACHIEVING INTIMACY:
God creates a provision for our need.

God wanted Adam, as well as us, to know that He created a need in mankind for relationships. Because of this need, God tells us that He will personally create a provision to uniquely correspond with our distinctive needs. Each of us must therefore admit our personal need before God and look to Him to meet this need.

5 DAILY WALK, DAY FIVE

1. Read Genesis 2:23 below:

    The man said, "This is now bone of my bones, and flesh of my flesh; She shall be called Woman, because she was taken out of Man."

    A paraphrase of this verse might be, "Wow! Where has she been all my life!!" Adam had never before seen an "Eve," yet he embraced her instantly. Why was he so elated?

    _____

    _____

2. How do you think it would affect your marriage if you began to look beyond your spouse's performance and would trust God to meet your need for intimacy?

    _____

    _____

    _____

3. Now read Genesis 2:24 below:

    Therefore shall a man leave his father and his mother, and shall cleave unto his wife: and they shall become one flesh (NASB).

In the space below, describe what you think God meant by:

Leave:

_____

Cleave:

_____

4. Read Genesis 2:25 below:

    And the man and his wife were both naked and were not ashamed.

    This verse implies that Adam and Eve were totally exposed to each other—physically, emotionally, and spiritually—without fear of rejection. Have you ever felt that level of intimacy with your spouse? If not, what do you think it would take to experience unqualified acceptance in your own marriage?

_____

_____

Step Four for Achieving Intimacy:
We believe and receive God's provision—our spouse.

Let's review God's four-step plan to achieving intimacy in marriage:

Four Steps in God's Meeting of Our Needs

Step One: God creates a need in our lives.

Step Two: God shows us our need.

Step Three: God creates the provision for our need.

Step Four: We receive God's provision.

Rejecting your spouse after marriage is simply doubting God and His provision in your life.

Sound simple? Try putting two imperfect, sinful people together under one roof. The problem comes when we begin to replace what God has already provided for us in our spouse with our desire for our spouse to perform according to our expectations in order to meet our needs.

In review, from week one:

FAITH PRINCIPLE NUMBER ONE:
By faith, we must commit ourselves to God's purposes of reflecting His image, reproducing a godly heritage, and reigning in spiritual warfare.

SO GOD'S SECOND FAITH-BASED PRINCIPLE FOR ONENESS IS:

By faith, we must receive our spouse

from God as His personal provision

for our individual needs.

✦ *Apply the Principle* ✦

1. Think back to a time when you have been critical of a weakness in your spouse. What really gets on your nerves? Now, as you read the five truths below, think how that weakness may actually be a blessing:

• God can meet your aloneness needs in spite of your spouse's weaknesses.

• One of God's major tools for changing your spouse with promised results is unconditional love.

• God actually uses your spouse's weaknesses as a tool to perfect your character.

• Your spouse's weaknesses are an opportunity for your strengths to be needed in his or her life.

• What you view as a weakness in your spouse today may indeed become a great blessing later in your marriage.

We believe that God can meet our needs with our spouse, not because he or she is perfect, but because God is. In fact, what we view as a weakness may be God's instrument to shape your character, provide you with opportunities to serve, or become a great blessing.

2.   This week write a love letter about how God has turned a perceived weakness in your spouse into a blessing in your life. Read them to each other over coffee. Be ready to share in class what this meant to you.

A QUICK LOOK BACK

A relationship based on performance rather than faith will create an unreal expectation of perfection in your spouse rather than trusting God for His provision. Instead of looking to your spouse to meet your needs, trust God that He has already met your needs through your spouse, with his or her strengths and weaknesses.

♥2 BECOMING ONE PRAYER

Heavenly Father, thank You for Your concern for my needs and marriage. I pray that I would possess the wisdom and faith to see You as the Creator of both my marriage and my spouse. Please forgive me for judging and looking to his or her performance in the past. I commit to receive my spouse as Your perfect provision for my aloneness need. Help me look beyond my spouse's weaknesses to You to meet my needs, heavenly Father. Give me the ability to love my spouse by faith as I hope in You. In the name of Jesus, Amen.

Complete the week two *Daily Walks* and small group discussion before reading these notes.

ONENESS: GOD'S GOAL FOR MARRIAGE

We've discussed how it's usually not until after the wedding day that our spouse's weaknesses come into focus. Eventually, when problems arise in the marriage, we are quick to blame our spouse rather than see our spouse as God's solution to the issues. Consequently, our hope of intimacy in marriage turns to irritation.

After working through God's purposes for oneness, most couples ask, "How do we find oneness for our marriage?" In Genesis 2, the Magna Carta of Marriage, God defines oneness and how we can experience it. Without a fundamental understanding of these extremely important passages, a couple may have trouble finding true biblical fulfillment in their relationship.

The definition of oneness is "being in agreement with God and His purposes and with one another."

First, we'll look at the four steps to obtaining oneness in your marriage.

GOD'S FOUR-STEP FORMULA FOR ONENESS IN MARRIAGE

The LORD God said, "It is not good for the man to be alone. I will make a helper suitable for him." Now the LORD God had formed out of the ground all the beasts of the field and all the birds of the air. He brought them to the man to see what he would name them; and whatever the man called each living creature, that was its name. So the man gave names to all the livestock, the birds of the air and all the beasts of the field. But for Adam no suitable helper was found. So the LORD God caused the man to fall into a deep sleep; and while he was sleeping, he took one of the man's ribs and closed up the place with flesh.

Then the LORD God made a woman from the rib He had taken out of the man, and He brought her to the man. The man said, "This is now bone of my bones and flesh of my flesh; she shall be called 'woman, ' for she was taken out of man."

For this reason a man will leave his father and mother and be united to his wife, and they will become one flesh. The man and his wife were both naked, and they felt no shame (Gen. 2:18-26).

At the time of creation, Adam had no sin. Adam also was in God's presence. He was in a perfect environment with no perceived need, yet God stated that Adam was alone. Though Christians often feel that God is the only absolute need in their lives, they should not, and God does not, minimize the importance of human relationships.

Step One—God creates each of us with an absolute need for relationships (Genesis 2:18).

When God said that it was not good for man to be alone, He was emphasizing to Adam (and all who would follow) that each person is created with a need for relationships. Therefore, God is responsible to create a spouse who corresponds uniquely to our needs just as He did with Adam's needs. Clearly, God wants us to look to Him for the fulfillment of our relationship needs.

Step Two—God shows each of us our need for relationship (Genesis 2:19–20).

God rarely gives us anything without first showing us our need. Instead of immediately creating Eve, God gave Adam the project of naming the ani-mals. As Adam named the animals, he discovered that there was no one that corresponded to him—no one to talk with, to eat with, and to love. Adam discovered he was alone.

Step Three—God creates a provision for our need (Genesis 2:21-22).

God caused Adam to sleep (total rest in dependence on God). When he awoke, the Scripture reports, God "brought her to the man." One would have expected Eve to be lying next to a sleeping Adam. By bringing Eve to Adam, God wanted Adam to know that He personally met the need that He created. *Just as Adam looked to God to meet his marital needs, so must we.*

Step Four—We believe and receive God's provision by faith (Genesis 2:23).

Adam trusted in God who had shown Himself faithful. When Adam gladly received Eve (Gen. 2:23), he had not "inspected" Eve, nor had she "performed" well. Instead, he received Eve based on who God was to him. God was faithful. God was good. Eve was a gift to him from a loving God. We too must receive our spouse with complete trust in God's goodness.

HOW GOD'S FOUR-STEP PLAN FOR ONENESS RELATES TO YOUR MARRIAGE

God meets our needs primarily through our spouse, but also through those in His Church and other friends. In the "God's Provision for Adam's Aloneness Needs" chart below, "Non-aloneness needs" refer to things such as food, clothing, shelter, and so on. "Aloneness needs" are always relational—our spouse first, followed by others such as children, friends, and family as well.

God creates this need in us to teach us dependence upon Himself and to equip us to reflect His image to an imperfect world. We can then reproduce a godly heritage and reign for Christ on this earth. God sought to protect us from Satan's sin of independence from

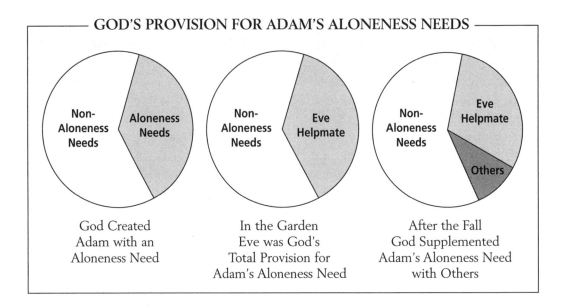

GOD'S PROVISION FOR ADAM'S ALONENESS NEEDS

Non-Aloneness Needs	Aloneness Needs

God Created
Adam with an
Aloneness Need

In the Garden
Eve was God's
Total Provision for
Adam's Aloneness Need

After the Fall
God Supplemented
Adam's Aloneness Need
with Others

God and designed us to trust Him daily to meet our aloneness needs. Therefore, He requires us to receive our spouse as a gift from Him.

Satan, on the other hand, wants us to view people—especially our spouse—as our problem instead of as God's provision (Ephesians 6:12). He wants us to isolate ourselves from the relationships God has provided for us, and ultimately to separate ourselves from God. If we keep our eyes on God and His Word, we need not fear our needs not being met, or the seeming weaknesses of our spouse.

God can meet our relational needs through our spouse's weaknesses.

Once people discover their spouse has weaknesses, they often believe it is a hindrance to oneness and intimacy. *Like Adam, by faith, you must receive your spouse as a provision from God.* Keep in mind that to reject your spouse in any way after marriage is to doubt God and His ability to provide for your needs. It impugns God's character and motives.

One important note here: If severe emotional, spiritual, or physical abuse exists in your marriage, you must seek immediate relief through professional Christian counsel. God can work miracles in your marriage, but in these cases it is imperative that you seek proper assistance.

GOD'S PRINCIPLE OF ONENESS RESULTS IN BLESSING

God established the principle of oneness (Genesis 2:24–25). The principle of oneness includes the idea that in marriage an old dependence ceases as one "leaves" his or her family of origin and their single status; a new relationship begins as the man trusts God and "cleaves" to his wife, and the two become "one flesh." To leave means "to untie, to break." To cleave means "to stick like glue." When we leave the old and cleave to the new we become "one flesh."

Our part is to leave; God's part is the cleaving, or joining together; and He says what He "has joined together let no man separate" (Mark 10:9, NASB). It is to be permanent. Marriage problems often arise because of a failure to leave or a failure to cleave.

If you were formerly divorced, or you were not a Christian when you married, or you just cannot be sure your spouse is your Eve or Adam, the principle of oneness still works for you. Scripture tells us that God hates divorce (Malachi 2:16), and He wants you to remain married. We also know from Scripture that God forgives past failures when they are confessed to Him (1 John 1:9). Do not let Satan confuse you or rob you of a wonderfully satisfying marriage. As you accept God's second faith principle: *by faith, we must receive our spouse from God as His personal provision for your individual needs,* then you will be able to better accomplish God's purposes for marriage: *reflect, reproduce,* and *reign.*

The principle of oneness results in a blessing. In Genesis 2:24-25, God states that Adam and Eve are to be one flesh. God says the man and his wife are free to be naked and unashamed. Certainly God is directly referring to physical nakedness, but in the context of all of Scripture, one can say that Adam and Eve were free to be totally exposed to each other and God, without fear. Emotionally, physically, intellectually, spiritually—in every way—they were exposed and unashamed.

Why were Adam and Eve able to be completely transparent with each other without any threat? Their transparency resulted from keeping their eyes on God instead of each other's performance, which always results in oneness.

Oneness can only be achieved if we believe that God designed our spouses (both their strengths and weaknesses) to help meet our deepest needs. In the beginning of Genesis, God laid out a four-step plan for obtaining oneness, so that we don't have to guess at how to achieve this goal.

The principle of oneness will truly rejuvenate your marriage and put you and your spouse on the right track toward fulfilling God's threefold purpose for your marriage: reflecting His image, reproducing godly children, reigning in spiritual warfare. As we progress through this study, you will see just how important oneness is to God and your marriage.

> Marriage problems often arise because of a failure to leave or a failure to cleave.

WEEK THREE:

God's Power for
ONENESS:
The Ministry of the Holy Spirit

But the Helper, the Holy Spirit,

whom the Father will send in My name,

He will teach you all things,

and bring to your remembrance all that I said to you

(JOHN 14:26, NASB).

GOD'S POWER FOR ONENESS

*H*ave you ever experienced marriage seminar meltdown? You come back from the seminar with a wheelbarrow full of notes, tapes, and proven principles, and surefire methods to put the spark back in your relationship. Your kids and friends notice a marked difference. You cuddle like high school sweethearts, you bring back your pet names, and you clear out Friday nights for a romantic rendezvous.

But after a few weeks, the dates are shoved out by long hours at the office and evenings chauffeuring the kids all over town, conversations go back to one-syllable discussions, and the spark starts to dim. What happened?

Marriage seminars are great. Sunday school classes on marriage are necessary. Tools like this small group study will give you proven principles for oneness. However, all the marriage wisdom in the world will only give you a road map; it won't drive you to oneness. Eventually couples realize they need more than a conference or a mountain of tools, they need power to change.

Moving from a *performance-based relationship* to a *faith-based relationship* takes more than great principles, it requires power. If you know Jesus Christ as your personal Savior, then you have the power. You just need to tap into it.

A QUICK LOOK AHEAD

Insanity has been defined as "continuing to do the same thing over and over again expecting different results." In marriage, we often want to change, but feel powerless to do so. We find ourselves ending up with the same arguments, the same hurt feelings, and the same dead ends.

Why is it so hard to get out of ruts in our marriage?
- Do we *know* enough?
- Are we *willing* to change?

In order to have a faith-based relationship, we need to have a supernatural power.

Last week we continued our journey from a *performance-based relationship* to a *faith-based relationship* by accepting our spouse as God's provision for oneness. This week we will take the next step, accepting by faith God's power for oneness.

 DAILY WALK, DAY ONE

Make sure you read last week's study notes before starting this section.
Review:

1. From your reading of last week's study notes, list the four steps for oneness found in Genesis 2:18-25:

_____

_____

_____

_____

2. How are you succeeding with understanding these four steps and their application to your marriage? How can you improve?

_____

_____

_____

3. On what basis did Adam accept Eve? Are you accepting your spouse in the same way? Give specific examples of where you fall short and what steps you have taken to improve your marriage in this area.

_____

_____

_____

_____

4. From Genesis 2:24, what two words does God use to establish a formula for oneness? What specific ways have you and your spouse implemented these two words into your marriage?

_____

_____

_____

✦ *Faith Steps* ✦

Remember, these exercises will not be discussed in class.

Part One (Personal)

Take some time to spend praying alone with God. Place a check in each box below as you pray about the following:

☐ Thanking God for my new understanding of His responsibility to meet my aloneness need through His provision.

☐ Confessing as sin to God any rejection of, withdrawal from, or bitterness toward my spouse. By faith, committing to God to receive my spouse as His personal provision for my aloneness need.

☐ Committing to God to trust Him with my spouse's weaknesses. By faith, choose to love him or her unconditionally, as you trust God for your own needs.

Part Two (Personal and as a Couple)

1. When we first met, the qualities that most attracted me to you were:

_____

_____

2. There are many qualities you have that I am thankful for in you (list favorite qualities of your spouse):

_____

_____

3. When I think of ways that at times I have been insensitive or failed you, I appreciate your patience with me. With God's help, I hope to improve. Thank you for enduring and waiting on me in … [name an area of insensitivity or failure you desire to work on]

_____

_____

4. From this time forward, God has led me to make the following commitments to you:

_____

_____

_____

5. My vision for the future of our marriage is:

_____

_____

_____

_____

Based on your answers above, write a love letter and share in class what this has meant to you to communicate your new commitments to your spouse. The better you communicate, the quicker God will be able to motivate and begin to change you and your spouse.

Then, before the date of your next small group meeting, schedule an hour together with your spouse, choosing a time and place that will allow for intimate communication. During your time, affectionately read to each other your statements contained in the love letters; then pray together, verbalizing your mutual commitment to the Lord.

  DAILY WALK, DAY TWO

Moving from a *performance-based relationship* to a *faith-based relationship* will require a supernatural power. On our own, we do not possess the power to change. Sure, we can change for a time, but we lack the power on our own to consistently pursue oneness like God intended. Think about your own responses to your spouse when he or she hurts you, doesn't meet your expectations, or disappoints you. Do you lash back in anger, stew in silence, or focus selfishly on your needs?

That's one reason why God sent the Holy Spirit into the life of each believer. Who is the Holy Spirit?

Before you begin your second daily journey, read chapter six in your companion book, Two Becoming One, *by Don and Sally Meredith.*

ATTRIBUTES OF THE HOLY SPIRIT

1. Look up each of the following Scriptures. From each verse, list a word or phrase that defines a particular attribute of the Holy Spirit. Look at what the Holy Spirit is doing or accomplishing in each verse.

Genesis 1:2:

_____

Psalm 139:7-8:

_____

Matthew 28:19:

_____

1 Corinthians 2:10-11:

_____

2. Pick one or two of these attributes that you think can help your pursuit of oneness right now:

_____

_____

3. Look up Ephesians 4:30. What can you tell about the Holy Spirit's personality from this verse?

_____

_____

_____

[3] DAILY WALK, DAY THREE

From our study above we see that the Holy Spirit is not simply a spirit. He is God Himself, a member of the Trinity. Now, let's study some of the specific ministries of the Holy Spirit.

ACTIVITIES OF THE HOLY SPIRIT

1. Look up the following Scriptures. From each verse, list the specific ways the Holy Spirit ministers to Christians:

John 16:7–8:

_____

Acts 1:8:

_____

Acts 10:19-20:

_____

Romans 8:13–14:

_____

1 Corinthians 2:12–13:

_____

2 Corinthians 1:3–4:

_____

Ephesians 5:18-21:

_____

Titus 3:4-6:

_____

2. How many of these ministries of the Holy Spirit have you experienced in your own life? As a couple? Give specific examples:

_____

_____

_____

_____

 # 4 DAILY WALK, DAY FOUR

In the past two days we have sought to understand the attributes and activities of the Holy Spirit. Now we need to learn how to release the power of the Holy Spirit's conviction, leading, teaching, and comfort in our lives and marriage.

From the Scriptures we study in this section, we will discover why it's so hard to change and move towards oneness.

1. Look up Galatians 5:16-17, 25; 1 John 1:3, 6, 9
   Define what it means to "live by the Spirit" (or "walk by the Spirit" in NASB) and have "fellowship with [God]":

   _____

   _____

   _____

   _____

   _____

2. Read Romans 7:21-24 below:

   I find then the principle that evil is present in me, the one who wants to do good. For I joyfully concur with the law of God in the inner man, but I see a different law in the members of my body, waging war against the law of my mind and making me a prisoner of the law of sin which is in my members. Wretched man that I am! Who will set me free from the body of this death?

   What internal battle rages within each believer? List some specific examples of how you have experienced this in your marriage:

   _____

   _____

   _____

   _____

   _____

3. Now study the passage from Romans 8:2-9 below:

   Through Christ Jesus the law of the Spirit of life set me free from the law of sin and death …. Those who live according to the sinful nature have their minds set on what that nature desires; but those who live in accordance with the Spirit have their minds set on what the Spirit desires. The mind of sinful man is death, but the mind controlled by the Spirit is life and peace…. You, however, are controlled not by the sinful nature but by the Spirit, if the Spirit of God lives in you.

   How does your sinful nature hinder you from the Holy Spirit working in your life?

   _____

   _____

   _____

One of the greatest indications that I am not depending on the Holy Spirit is the absence of power in my life.

4. Read Ephesians 4:29-30 below:

Let no unwholesome word proceed from your mouth, but only such a word as is good for edification according to the need of the moment, so that it will give grace to those who hear. Do not grieve the Holy Spirit of God, by whom you were sealed for the day of redemption.

How do you "grieve" the Holy Spirit in your marriage? Have you done that this week? If so, what steps have you taken to yield to the convicting power of the Holy Spirit?

_____

_____

_____

_____

[5] DAILY WALK, DAY FIVE

Let's continue to examine the practical issues most marriages face, as our sinful nature—our flesh—tries to exercise power in our lives. In all of our struggles between the flesh and the Spirit, only if we continue to yield to the Holy Spirit will we experience oneness in marriage.

1. Study each passage below. State how each source may have negatively affected your marriage.

Satan (John 8:44)

_____

_____

The world (1 John 2:15–17)

_____

_____

The flesh (Galatians 5:19–21)

_____

_____

2. Look up Galatians 5:22–23 and list the fruit of the Spirit below. Why is the fruit of the Spirit important to oneness in marriage? Why do you think some couples uniquely exhibit these qualities while most do not?

_____

_____

_____

_____

_____

How can you better apply the fruit of the Spirit to the struggles you listed above?

_____

_____

3. Read Romans 13:14 below:

But put on the Lord Jesus Christ, and make no provision for the flesh in regard to its lusts.

When we feel the temptation to yield to the sinful nature, how should we respond?

_____

_____

4. Read 1 John 1:9 below:

If we confess our sins, He is faithful and righteous to forgive us our sins and to cleanse us from all unrighteousness.

When we do yield to the flesh, and we will at times, what should our immediate response be?

_____

_____

5. In marriage, when we sin against our spouse, we should be quick to seek their forgiveness as well (read James 5:16 and Ephesians 4:26-27). On a scale of 1-10, "1" being easy and "10" being difficult, how hard is it for you to apologize and seek forgiveness from your spouse? Why is that?

_____

_____

_____

_____

In review, from week one:

FAITH PRINCIPLE NUMBER ONE:

By faith, we must commit ourselves to God's purposes of reflecting His image, reproducing a godly heritage, and reigning in spiritual warfare.

In review, from week one:

FAITH PRINCIPLE NUMBER TWO:

By faith, we must receive our spouse from God as His personal provision for our individual needs.

THEREFORE, GOD'S **THIRD** FAITH-BASED PRINCIPLE FOR ONENESS IS:

By faith, we must

daily commit to release the power of the

Holy Spirit in our lives.

✥ *Apply the Principle* ✥

Talk to any general, and he will tell you that a key to success in war is planning and preparation. Daily, we find ourselves locked in battles between our flesh and the Holy Spirit in our lives. Unfortunately most of us never take the time to prepare or plan for the upcoming battles.

God provides a plan for us in Romans 12:1-2 below:

Therefore I urge you, brethren, by the mercies of God, to present your bodies a living and holy sacrifice, acceptable to God, which is your spiritual service of worship. And do not be conformed to this world, but be transformed by the renewing of your mind, so that you may prove what the will of God is, that which is good and acceptable and perfect.

How does God tell us to counter the pressures to conform to this world?

_____

_____

How are you tempted to "yield to the flesh" in your marriage?

_____

_____

Develop a plan for renewing your mind rather than conforming again to your sinful desires when that battle comes.

Possible ideas:

- Memorize Scripture related to your struggle.
- Find an accountability partner on this issue.
- Write out a faith commitment to your spouse now and act on that when the temptation hits.

A QUICK LOOK BACK

The main reason we remain powerless to change our marriages is because we consistently yield to our sinful natures rather than to the power of the Spirit. Though we may know God's purposes and provision for oneness, unless we tap into God's power for oneness, we will sink back into a performance-based relationship. However, if we choose to consistently yield to the Spirit, we will move towards truly living out God's purposes for our marriage. Only then will we be able to accept our spouse as God's provision for our aloneness needs.

 BECOMING ONE PRAYER

Heavenly Father, thank You for sending the Holy Spirit to comfort and to teach me. Forgive me, Father, for grieving the Holy Spirit when I yield to my sinful and selfish nature. By faith, I now choose to let the Holy Spirit control and empower me from this point forward. When I sin in the future, I commit to immediately confess my sin and continue to let the Holy Spirit control my life. Thank You for Your tremendous provision of Your Spirit. In the name of Jesus, Amen.

Complete the week three *Daily Walks* and small group discussion before reading these notes.

THE HOLY SPIRIT: GOD'S POWER FOR A FAITH-BASED MARRIAGE

While marriage seminars and Sunday school classes fill your head up with knowledge and the principles of marriage, the power to fix your marriage often remains conspicuously absent.

After Christ ascended into heaven, the Holy Spirit, or "Counselor," became our source for knowing God and succeeding in life and marriage (see John 16:7, 13a). The Holy Spirit is greatly concerned about your marriage. When you respond to your spouse based on performance: holding grudges, lashing out in anger, or expecting perfection, then you grieve the Holy Spirit. Couples who desire to please God in their marriage will need to consistently yield to the Spirit's promptings in their lives. An outline of the attributes and ministry of the Holy Spirit follows.

Husbands and wives must recognize the attributes of the Holy Spirit before they can understand His ministry in their marriage. The Holy Spirit is God and desires for us to be one with our spouse. Once you realize this, it is much easier to trust the Holy Spirit and to let Him work in your marriage.

THE ATTRIBUTES OF THE HOLY SPIRIT

The Holy Spirit is God (Matthew 28:19).

The Holy Spirit is not a subset of God; He is God. As such, He possesses divine attributes as a member of the Trinity:

• The Holy Spirit is omnipresent (present everywhere; Psalm 139:7–8).

• The Holy Spirit is omniscient (all-knowing; 1 Corinthians 2:10–11).

• The Holy Spirit is omnipotent (all-powerful; Genesis 1:2).

The Holy Spirit has a personality and can be related to personally.

The Spirit is not so distant from us that He is not touched personally by our actions:

• The Holy Spirit has feelings (Ephesians 4:30).

• The Holy Spirit can be obeyed or disobeyed (Acts 10:19–20).

THE ACTIVITIES OF THE HOLY SPIRIT

At the moment we receive Jesus Christ as our personal Savior, the Holy Spirit comes into our lives permanently. This is often referred to as the "indwelling" of the Spirit (Romans 8:9). As the Spirit enters our lives, He does a number of works to produce a living fellowship between God and us. Of course, these works also affect the relationships we have with others around us, particularly our spouse and our children.

The Holy Spirit is our means to achieve personal fellowship with God.

Fellowship is an intimate mutual communication (see 1 John 1:3–4). Successful marriages are engaged in an intimate fellowship with God through the work of the Holy Spirit.

We choose to accept the Holy Spirit's ministry.

Accepting Christ as Savior does not necessarily mean that the Holy Spirit is in control of your life. You must commit your will and give the control to the Holy Spirit so that the life of Christ may be manifested in you. "Offer your bodies as living sacrifices, holy and pleasing to God—this is your spiritual act of worship" (Romans 12:1). Though we have a choice to accept or reject the ministry of the Holy Spirit, we can never live the full Christian life apart from the control of the Holy Spirit.

The Holy Spirit helps daily in our fellowship with God and others.

Although we cannot live the Christian life by ourselves, we do have the power to live a life that reflects Christ because the Holy Spirit indwells us. Successful marriages depend on the power of the Holy Spirit:

- The Holy Spirit gives us power to be Christ-like (Ephesians 3:16).
- The Holy Spirit directs our lives on a daily basis (Romans 8:14).
- The Holy Spirit convicts us of sin (John 16:8).
- The Holy Spirit empowers us to fight sin in our lives (Galatians 5:15–16).
- The Holy Spirit causes our marriages to glorify Christ (John 16:14).

The Holy Spirit came to glorify Christ. If couples yield to the ministry of the Holy Spirit in their lives, their marriages will lift up Christ and make Him known by their words and deeds.

> Fellowship with God is not optional if we want to succeed in marriage.

Living by the Spirit is what the Bible calls "fellowship."

Fellowship with God—that special intimate communication with Him—is not optional if we want to succeed in marriage. Scripture describes this daily fellowship as "living" or "walking" (NASB) in the Spirit (Galatians 5:16). Because sin drives us away from each other and God, couples who desire to be one should aggressively learn to walk by the Spirit of God to avoid gratifying their sinful natures.

The Holy Spirit bestows blessings.

The results of "walking in the Spirit" will be the nine aspects of the fruit of the Spirit (Galatians 5:22–23), including love, joy, and peace. The Bible promises love—the very hope of every marriage. We need to yield to the Holy Spirit's power on a daily basis in order to exhibit this fruit. Only the Spirit of God can consistently produce this fruit in their lives.

THE HOLY SPIRIT'S IMPACT CAN BE SHORT-CIRCUITED BY LACK OF FAITH AND BY DISOBEDIENCE.

Christians do not experience the full power of the Holy Spirit in their lives and marriages because of two primary factors: sin and lack of faith.

Husbands and wives block God's power and fellowship when they sin.

Though God saves us from our sin, He does not automatically save us from the temptation of our sinful nature. Once we come to know Him, we start on an internal battle between our "flesh" (sinful nature) and the "Spirit" (God's Holy Spirit). With every decision, we are faced with a choice: yield to the flesh, or yield to the Spirit. When we yield to the "flesh" we move towards *performance* in our relationships. But when we yield to the Holy Spirit, we move towards a *faith-based relationship.* Depending on how we yield will ultimately determine our success or failure in marriage.

Sin can block both God's power and our fellowship with Him

(1 John 1:5–6). Just as walking in the Spirit produces good fruit, walking in the flesh produces bad fruit, including "discord, jealousy, fits of rage, selfish ambition, dissensions, factions, and envy" (Galatians 5:19–21). It is not God's desire for marriages to be characterized by such deeds. Sin blocks the Holy Spirit's power to bless and produce the desired fruit of oneness.

Husbands and wives block God's power and fellowship by lacking faith.

The Bible clearly exhorts us to fellowship with God and to walk by the Spirit. However, hearing these exhortations is not enough. Couples must act on these exhortations by faith. Without faith, we cannot please God (Hebrews 11:6). We must believe that God the Father, God the Son, and God the Holy Spirit exist and that God can make a difference in our marriages. We must believe that He can give us the power to have a successful marriage.

THE HOLY SPIRIT RESTORES FELLOWSHIP WHEN HUSBANDS AND WIVES WALK BY THE SPIRIT.

Acting apart from faith and in sinful disobedience is what the Bible calls "grieving the Holy Spirit" (Ephesians 4:30). Consider the chart on page. 59, "An Individual's Different Choices of Will." The three circles depict three kinds of lives.

In each circle (life), the throne represents the person's will, the control or decision-making center of his life. The cross represents Christ, while the "S" represents self. The black dots inside the circle represent different interests and activities in life. Notice that when sin reigns, the Christian no longer has Christ in charge, and the activities of life are scattered and without meaning.

Confession of sin restores fellowship and our walk by the Spirit.

God knew husbands and wives would struggle with sin. Because He loves us, He provides a way to deal with sin: "If we confess our sins, he is faithful and just and will forgive us our sins and purify us from all unright-eousness" (1 John 1:9). By God's grace, when we confess our sin, God imme-diately cleanses us and restores us to fellowship. This faith step allows us to once again take advantage of God's power in our lives and marriages.

Prayer empowers the Holy Spirit in our lives.

For oneness in your marriage, you must trust not only that God, through the Holy Spirit, can transform your marriage but also that He can act on your behalf. Praying opens the door of your marriage to the power the Holy Spirit. We note four elements in prayer, which can lead your marriage toward a renewed sense of oneness:

1. Ask God to teach you these insights concerning His Holy Spirit.

2. Believe that God loves you and that He desires to walk with you in oneness through the power of the Holy Spirit.

3. Confess to God your utter dependency on the Holy Spirit for power. If there is any known sin in your life, confess it by agreeing with God that it is sin and is displeasing to Him.

4. Draw upon God's power by faith and obedience. Begin walking by the Spirit in your marriage. "Since we live by the Spirit, let us keep in step with the Spirit" (Galatians 5:25). Be a couple centered on Christ, not a couple centered on self.

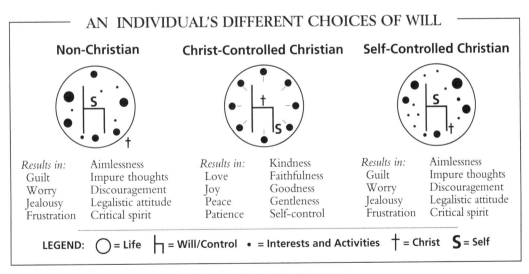

AN INDIVIDUAL'S DIFFERENT CHOICES OF WILL

Non-Christian

Results in:
Guilt
Worry
Jealousy
Frustration

Aimlessness
Impure thoughts
Discouragement
Legalistic attitude
Critical spirit

Christ-Controlled Christian

Results in:
Love
Joy
Peace
Patience

Kindness
Faithfulness
Goodness
Gentleness
Self-control

Self-Controlled Christian

Results in:
Guilt
Worry
Jealousy
Frustration

Aimlessness
Impure thoughts
Discouragement
Legalistic attitude
Critical spirit

LEGEND: ◯ = Life   ⊢ = Will/Control   • = Interests and Activities   † = Christ   S = Self

Source: *Have You Made the Wonderful Discovery of the Spirit Filled Life?*
©1995, New Life publishers, Campus Crusade for Christ. Used by permission.

THE HOLY SPIRIT IS AVAILABLE ONLY TO CHRISTIANS. ARE YOU A CHRISTIAN?

Our discussion of the Holy Spirit assumes every husband and wife reading this is a Christian. Without a personal relationship with Jesus Christ, the Holy Spirit is unavailable. So ask yourself a vital question at this point: Am I absolutely sure that I am a Christian?

Maybe you grew up in a Christian home or are a member of a local church. And, of course, you are now involved in a Christian small group study. But none of these things actually means that you are a Christian, and the success of this study is dependent upon one being a Christian.

Look at the diagram entitled "A Couple's Different Choices of Will." Which one of those three settings honestly represents your marriage? If you alone or as a couple are on the throne and Christ is outside the

> Scripture tells us that the way to salvation and the way to know that we are Christians is to accept Christ into our lives as our Lord and Savior—He is the way to God.

circle of your life, as the "non-Christian" diagram indicates, then you need to take a moment and ask Christ into your life, thanking Him for dying for all of your sins. This moment will change the rest of your life and lead you to fulfillment beyond your imagination. If Christ is inside the circle but off the throne, the self-centered life will hinder your relationship with your spouse and your fellowship with God.

Scripture tells us that the way to salvation and the way to know that we are Christians is to accept Christ into our lives as our Lord and Savior; He is the way to God. The Bible states we are all sinners and are separated from God: "For all have sinned and fall short of the glory of God" (Romans 3:23). The Bible also states that sin leads to death: "For the

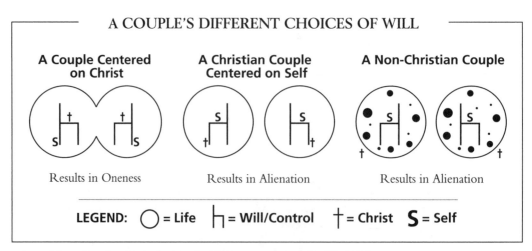

A COUPLE'S DIFFERENT CHOICES OF WILL

A Couple Centered on Christ

Results in Oneness

A Christian Couple Centered on Self

Results in Alienation

A Non-Christian Couple

Results in Alienation

LEGEND: ◯ = Life   ⊓ = Will/Control   † = Christ   **S** = Self

Adapted from *Have You Made the Wonderful Discovery of the Spirit Filled Life?*
©1995, New Life publishers, Campus Crusade for Christ. Used by permission.

wages of sin is death, but the gift of God is eternal life in Christ Jesus our Lord" (Romans 6:23).

The Gospel so clearly presented by Jesus in John 3:16–17 remains the same today: "For God so loved the world that He gave His one and only Son, that whoever believes in Him shall not perish but have eternal life. For God did not send His Son into the world to condemn the world, but to save the world through Him." Jesus said He is the only way to God: "I am the way and the truth and the life. No one comes to the Father except through Me" (John 14:6).

To give your life to Christ, pray this prayer, and believe that Christ will hear you and honor your desire to become one with Him.

PRAYER OF SALVATION

Dear heavenly Father, I have sinned against You and have lived my life far apart from You. I ask that You would forgive me for all of the sins that I have committed. Father, I come before You humbly today, desiring to receive Christ as my personal Lord and Savior. I confess that He is the only way to salvation, the only way to You. Thank You, Lord Jesus, for dying for me and that You are now alive and ready and willing to transform my life. Lord, I trust You to keep Your word that whoever believes on the name of Christ shall not perish but have eternal life. Thank You. In the name of Jesus, Amen.

If you have said that prayer, congratulations! You have made a confession of faith, and according to Scripture, your salvation is sure and absolute (John 10:28–29; 1 John 5:11–12). We urge you to do three things.

First, tell your small group leader about your decision. He or she will be able to encourage you and answer some of your questions.

Second, find a church that will teach you from the Bible.

Finally, pray that the Holy Spirit will fill you with wisdom and knowledge, and ask for guidance to find others who will help you strengthen your newfound faith in Christ (Colossians 1:9-14).

If you are a believer, you possess the power to achieve oneness because the Spirit lives inside of you. If by faith, we live by the Spirit and not our performance-minded flesh, then we will see God's marriage principles turn into marriage practices.

WEEK FOUR:

God's Instruments for
CHANGE:
Love and Blessing

Do nothing out of selfish ambition or vain conceit,

but in humility consider others better than yourselves.

Each of you should look not only to your

own interests, but also to the interests of others

(Philippians 2:3–4).

God's Instruments of Change

When was the last time your spouse hurt you? If you can't remember, then you're either just about to say, "I do," or you're living in denial. Two sinful people living under one roof can be a volatile mix. So, when was the last time you felt betrayed or slighted by your bride or groom? Was it an insult? A snide remark? A sarcastic comment about your cooking in front of friends? Maybe it was your husband watching the game on the night of your anniversary. Or maybe you're engaged in an ongoing barrage of verbal barbs, or even just feeling neglected or unappreciated.

Now that you are thinking about how you didn't deserve to be treated with such callousness, think about how you responded. Did you return insult for insult? Did you hide the pain behind a veil of bitterness? Or did you find a way to "get even"?

Why do marriages turn into insult battlefields rather than blessing oases like you dreamt about and God intended? Most couples answer that question identically: "It's my spouse's fault. If I could just change them, my marriage would be great." But the Bible offers a much different solution.

A QUICK LOOK AHEAD

Did you know that nowhere in the Bible are we told to change other people? Change *our* own actions? Yes. Change *our* own attitudes? Certainly. But the moment we start down the road to changing our spouse, we're destined for a dead end. If we go there, we are setting ourselves and our spouse up for defeat.

Perhaps the greatest indication of whether or not we have a *performance-based relationship* is if we act on our natural impulses to change our spouse:

- "But you don't know my husband, he cares more about his cars than his kids."
- "I'm just giving back what my wife dishes out. Once she admits her fault, I'll be happy to admit mine."
- "He stopped loving me a long time ago."
- "She *always* complains. I can never do anything right in her eyes."

How do you try to change your spouse?

- Through manipulation?
- Through guilt?
- Through anger?
- Through a "holier than thou" attitude?
- Through the "silent treatment"?

Last week we learned that in order to have a *faith-based relationship,* we need to accept by faith the supernatural power of the Holy Spirit. The toughest part of yielding to the Spirit is when our flesh cries out for retribution and the Spirit tells us to do the exact opposite. Only when we yield to the Spirit's urges will we change. This week, as we discover God's fourth faith principle for oneness, we will highlight two proven methods for changing your spouse.

1 DAILY WALK, DAY ONE

Make sure you read last week's study notes before starting this section.
Review:

1. Why is it important to understand the ministry of the Holy Spirit in order to reflect God's image as a couple?

_____

_____

_____

2. Where do you struggle with "walking in the Spirit" in your marriage?

_____

_____

_____

3. Why do we need to "yield to the Spirit" in order to achieve oneness?

_____

_____

_____

✦ Faith Steps ✦

Remember, these exercises will not be discussed in class.

As an application of last week's material, this may be one of the most important projects in this workbook. Do not skip this exercise. Understanding the work of the Holy Spirit will not only change your marriage, but your personal life as well.

Part One (Personal)

In Galatians 5:16–23, we learn that our flesh sets its desires against the desires of the Holy Spirit. If the flesh is dominant in our lives, undesirable behavior results. On the other hand, if we allow the Holy Spirit to lead our lives, our lives will be characterized by the fruit of the Holy Spirit. The purpose of part one is to help us determine the works or fruit that now characterize our lives and marriages.

In the chart below, circle the number that most accurately represents how frequently the characteristics listed on the left appear in your marriage and in your activities or attitudes outside the marriage. Use the following scale:

1= never, 2= rarely, 3= sometimes, 4= often, and 5= always

CHARACTERISTICS	INSIDE YOUR MARRIAGE RELATIONSHIP	OUTSIDE YOUR MARRIAGE RELATIONSHIP
Immorality	1 2 3 4 5	1 2 3 4 5
Impure Thoughts	1 2 3 4 5	1 2 3 4 5
Lust	1 2 3 4 5	1 2 3 4 5
Occult/horoscopes	1 2 3 4 5	1 2 3 4 5
Hatred	1 2 3 4 5	1 2 3 4 5
Fighting	1 2 3 4 5	1 2 3 4 5
Jealousy	1 2 3 4 5	1 2 3 4 5

CHARACTERISTICS	INSIDE YOUR MARRIAGE RELATIONSHIP					OUTSIDE YOUR MARRIAGE RELATIONSHIP				
Outbursts of Anger	(1)	2	3	4	5	(1)	2	3	4	5
Greed	(1)	2	3	4	5	(1)	2	3	4	5
Complaining	1	2	(3)	4	5	1	2	(3)	4	5
Criticism	(1)	2	3	4	5	(1)	2	3	4	5
Envying	1	2	(3)	4	5	1	2	3	(4)	5
Drunkenness	(1)	2	3	4	5	(1)	2	3	4	5
Carousing	(1)	2	3	4	5	(1)	2	3	4	5
Love	1	2	3	(4)	5	1	2	(3)	4	5
Joy	1	2	(3)	4	5	1	2	3	(4)	5
Peace	1	2	3	(4)	5	1	2	3	4	5
Patience	1	2	(3)	4	5	1	(2)	3	4	5
Kindness	1	2	(3)	4	5	1	(2)	3	4	5
Goodness	1	2	(3)	4	5	1	2	3	4	5
Faithfulness	1	2	3	(4)	5	1	2	3	4	5
Gentleness	1	2	3	(4)	5	1	2	3	4	5
Self-Control	1	2	3	(4)	5	1	2	(3)	4	5

The focus is your behavior both inside and outside your marriage.

Total the numbers for the "acts of the sinful nature," or "deeds of the flesh," shown in regular type. Then total the numbers for the fruit of the Spirit, shown in italics. There should be a reverse relationship—a high score in the fruit of the Spirit should mean a low score in the works of the flesh, since the Scripture says as we "live by the Spirit" we "will not gratify the desires of the sinful nature" (Galatians 5:16). If you scored 30 or more on the final nine characteristics (in italics), the fruit of the Spirit ought to be evident in your life. Unless you scored over 35, however, you need to allow the Holy Spirit to further empower your marriage.

Part Two (Personal)

Most people desire a marriage that exhibits the fruit of the Holy Spirit, yet Part One may have shown such fruit to be limited in your marriage and life.

The purpose of Part Two is to take steps that will help us yield to the power of the Holy Spirit.

Step One: Confess known sin.
Read 1 John 1:9 below:

If we confess our sins, He is faithful and righteous to forgive us our sins and to cleanse us from all unrighteousness.

Since sin blocks the power of the Holy Spirit, each of us must confess our sins to God. We must agree with God that what we did was wrong.

What sins do you need to confess to God right now? Review the chart above concerning deeds done in the flesh. Release any guilt to Him and thank Him for forgiving you. Then thank Him for not just forgiving but forgetting your sin (according to Psalm 103:10–12).

Step Two: Give the control of your life to God to do His will.
Read Romans 12:1-2 below:

Therefore I urge you, brethren, by the mercies of God, to present your bodies a living and holy sacrifice, acceptable to God, which is your spiritual service of worship. And do not be conformed to this world, but be transformed by the renewing of your mind, so that you may prove what the will of God is, that which is good and acceptable and perfect.

When we become Christians, the Holy Spirit comes to live in us forever. He doesn't control us, however, until we give that control to Him. Many Christians are living powerless, defeated lives because they don't yield that control. But God gives us a marvelous formula for living a full and purposeful life. Presenting our bodies to God involves our past (all that has taken place—good or bad), our present (including our family, career, material possessions), and our future (all of our fears, hope and dreams).

If God promises that His will is good for us, will be pleasing to us, and is perfect for us, what more could we ask for? To give God everything is really the best and most reasonable thing any Christian can do. As you do, peace will reign in your mind and heart.

Step Three: Walk by faith in the power of the Holy Spirit.

Christ emphasized that the Holy Spirit is our Helper in living the Christian life. Christians are to walk in the power of the Holy Spirit (Galatians 5:16, 25). After confessing any known sin and yielding control of your life to God, all a Christian must do to activate the Holy Spirit is to believe that the Holy Spirit is truly available and then step out and begin to walk in the Spirit. This is called faith, and only faith will please God (Hebrews 11:6).

Right now, activate the Holy Spirit in your life by praying the following prayer:

Dear Father, I need You. I acknowledge that I have been directing my own life and that, as a result, I have sinned against You. I thank You that You have forgiven my sins through Christ's death on the cross for me. I now invite Christ to take His rightful place on the throne of my life. I give You my past, my present, and my future. Take control of my life through the power of Your Holy Spirit. As an expression of my faith, I now thank You for directing my life and for controlling me with Your Holy Spirit. In the name of Jesus, Amen.

Part Three (Complete as a Couple)

The purpose of Part Three is to release the power of the Holy Spirit in your marriage. In an atmosphere of love and communication, complete the following steps before your next small group meeting.

• Review with your spouse what you have learned about the Holy Spirit.

• Share with each other the decisions you have made and express your desire to walk in the Spirit in your marriage.

• While holding hands, take turns praying. Express to God your desire to walk in the Spirit in your marriage. Then agree together that from this point forward you will walk in the Spirit together as each of you allows the Holy Spirit to lead your life.

2 DAILY WALK, DAY TWO

Before you begin your second daily journey, read chapter seven in your companion book, Two Becoming One, *by Don and Sally Meredith.*

It's natural for husbands and wives to try and change one another. Yet nowhere in Scripture are we told to change other people. Rather, Scripture reveals that God ordains only two forces for changing one's spouse: the *active force of love* and the *reactive force of blessing*—both manifested through the Holy Spirit's power in us.

Let's first take a look at the active force of love. Since love is God's active force for change, let's define it in order to gain a clear understanding.

1. The call of Scripture is to go beyond romantic (*eros*) and friendship (*philos*) love to a more enduring (*agape*) love. From the following verses that describe agape love, how would you define this love?

Luke 6:27-28, 31-36

Doing good no matter what comes against us —
NO MATTER WHAT
His unmerited favor toward us
warrants unmerited mercy toward others mercy + grace

1 John 4:7–11

God loved us sent Jesus to redeem our naturally sinful selves back to him we ought to love one another

1 Corinthians 13:4-7

Love never fails

2. What are some keys to loving with *agape* love?

Remembering we were loved when we were yet sinners so undeserving of love - who are we to withhold love from another

3. What is your biggest hurdle to applying this type of love in your marriage?

no hurdle

[3] DAILY WALK, DAY THREE

Agape love is the active force that God uses as an instrument of change in our marriages. It is the type of love that will help lead you and your spouse into a faith-based relationship, and it is the only love referred to in Scripture with promises attached to it. Let's take a closer look at what Scripture tells us about *agape* love.

1. The *agape* love referred to in the following verses implies certain results. List the results you can observe.

Ephesians 5:25–29

man loves his wife like Christ loves the church honoring here loving her as he does himself

1 John 4:18

no fear

2.   Why are these implied results important to your marriage?

it is how honoring is evident not through fear, but revering each other

3.   In week two, we learned that couples must receive each other as God's perfect provision for their needs. How does *agape* love help us to fulfill these faith commitments required in marriage?

love covers a multitude of sin.

> When you tell your spouse, "I love you," ask yourself what you truly mean. Are you *referring to* eros, philos, *or* agape *love? Only* agape *love will release the full power of God's love in your marriage. Such sacrificial love takes faith, but over time it produces more faith, causing your spouse to become freed up from performance as well as becoming more beautiful on both the inside and the outside.*

[4] DAILY WALK, DAY FOUR

Many couples live in an insult-for-insult environment where retaliation is a way of life. How can we expect positive changes in our spouse if we are constantly trading insults? It's impossible. Let's look at God's alternative.

The word revenge is not in God's marriage vocabulary. Instead, if you want to release His power for change, Scripture says to return a blessing when you are insulted. *God promises to not only change your spouse, but to bless you as well.* In the homework for days four and five, we will define insult and blessing, and then discover God's second force for change: the reactive force of blessing.

1.   The Bible provides examples of the many insults that can occur in relationships. Study the following passages, and after each verse, indicate what way(s) of insulting another person is (are) being described. The first two have been done as examples.

Proverbs 22:12:
being unfaithful or contentious; treacherous

Proverbs 26:21:
strife with words; quarrelsome

Proverbs 27:15–16:

Complaining whining

Matthew 5:22:

anger insulting, putting people down

Galatians 5:19–21:

sexual immorality, shameful things

Ephesians 5:4:

filthy talk, foolish talk, evil talk

James 3:5–10:

curses, (evil, deadly poison)

James 3:14–15:

Jealousy

2. How do these insults affect your marriage?

tear it down, create havoc and destruction feed into division

3. The Bible also provides many examples of blessings that can take place in relationships. Study the following passages, and below each verse, list as many ways to bless your spouse as you can observe.

Where there is no guidance the people fall, but in abundance of counselors there is victory (PROVERBS 11:14).

I thank my God every time I remember you (PHILIPPIANS 1:3).

thanksgiving for you, who you are

As for me, far be it from me that I should sin against the Lord by failing to pray for you. And I will teach you the way that is good and right (1 SAMUEL 12:23).

In praying for you —

Each spouse must make a willful decision to return a blessing in spite of the hurt just experienced.

If you, then, though you are evil, know how to give good gifts to your children, how much more will your Father in heaven give good gifts to those who ask Him (MATTHEW 7:11).

You are God's good gift to me —

Do nothing out of selfish ambition or vain conceit, but in humility consider others better than yourselves. Each of you should look not only to your own interests, but also to the interests of others (PHILIPPIANS 2:3–4).

I love sharing this with you

How beautiful you are, my darling, how beautiful you are! Your eyes are like doves. How handsome you are, my beloved, and so pleasant! Indeed, our couch is luxuriant! (SONG OF SOLOMON 1:15–16).

You are still my dearly best beloved!

4. Have you given your spouse any positive affirmation (blessing) this week? If so, describe your actions. If not, do it now!

Yes for making a good decision

5 DAILY WALK, DAY FIVE

Because the natural human impulse is to seek revenge when wronged, revenge is one of the toughest areas for couples to overcome. For some, revenge looks like an angry outburst, for others it is a silent punishment of the one who wronged. Though many marriages eventually succumb to revenge, God is very clear about where He stands on this issue.

It is important to note, that your struggle in marriage is against Satan, not your spouse (Ephesians 6:12). Let's take a closer look at revenge and God's alternative: the reactive force of blessing.

1. Read Luke 6:28 and Romans 12:9–21. Based on these verses, how do you think God views revenge? Does Scripture list any exceptions to God's statements concerning revenge?

Bless those who use you + plan evil for you
Defeat evil by doing good

God says he will do it in Gen 12 bless those who bless you and curse those who curse you!

You meant it for evil but God used it for good

2. Read 1 Peter 3:8–12 below:

To sum up, all of you be harmonious, sympathetic, brotherly, kindhearted, and humble in spirit; not returning evil for evil or insult for insult, but giving a blessing instead; for you were called for the very purpose that you might inherit a blessing. For, "The one who desires life, to love and see good days, must keep his tongue from evil and his lips from speaking deceit. He must turn away from evil and do good; he must seek peace and pursue it. For the eyes of the Lord are toward the righteous, And His ears attend to their prayer, but the face of the Lord is against those who do evil."

List reasons, stated or implied, that it is better to return a blessing than an insult when wronged.

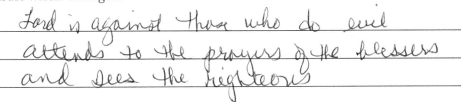

Lord is against those who do evil
attends to the prayers of the blessers
and sees the righteous

3. Think of some practical ways you can return a blessing for an insult.

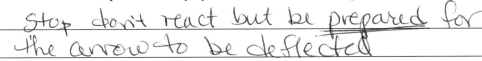

Stop don't react but be prepared for
the arrow to be deflected

4. Summarize how the active force of love and the reactive force of blessing can enable positive changes in your spouse.

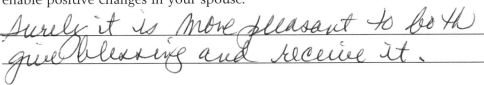

Surely it is more pleasant to both
give blessing and receive it.

In week one we learned:

FAITH PRINCIPLE NUMBER **ONE**:
> *By faith, we must commit ourselves to God's purposes*
> *of reflecting His image, reproducing a godly heritage,*
> *and reigning in spiritual warfare.*

In week two we learned:

FAITH PRINCIPLE NUMBER TWO:

By faith, we must receive our spouse from God as His personal provision for our individual needs.

In week three we learned:

FAITH PRINCIPLE NUMBER THREE:

By faith, we must daily commit to release the power of the Holy Spirit in our lives.

THEREFORE, GOD'S FOURTH FAITH-BASED PRINCIPLE FOR ONENESS IS:

By faith, we must submit to the only active and reactive biblical forces for change in marriage: agape love and blessing.

⇥ *Apply the Principle* ⇤

One of the most practical verses in all of Scripture is Ephesians 4:26:

Be angry, and yet do not sin; do not let the sun go down on your anger.

Notice that it does not say, "don't ever get angry." The Bible says, in our anger, don't sin. Our spouse will hurt us. Often times it may lead to anger. But if we respond with *agape* love rather than retaliation, we can move towards resolution rather than revenge.

Also, you will see that we are to never to go to bed mad. This doesn't mean, "stay up and fight!" This means that we should seek a resolution quickly rather than letting unresolved anger fester. If resolution needs more time, schedule it for the following day.

Are there opportunities for you to actively apply agape love in your marriage right now? Instead of bunkering down in bitterness, why not find a way to bless your spouse before you turn out the light? Here are some steps for resolution:

1. Seek forgiveness from God for any anger or bitterness that is in your own heart.

2. Verbally affirm your commitment and love for your spouse.

3. Take "always" and "never" out of your vocabulary. Make the object of your discussion a specific situation where you were hurt rather than the spouse. For example, rather than saying, "You *never* make me feel special," say, "It has been a couple of weeks since you and I had time alone, I really would like some special time with you."

4. Come to a unified resolution.

5. Pray together for renewed commitment.

A QUICK LOOK BACK

There is a way to respond to our spouse, but it's with divinely inspired ammunition — *agape* love and blessing. Until we intentionally yield to the Spirit and release God's two forces of change—the active force of *agape* love and the reactive force of blessing—then our efforts to change our spouse will be in vain. Instead of inspiring oneness, we will widen the chasm of separation in our marriages.

Heavenly Father, I confess to You that I have been manipulative and selfish toward my spouse in the past. At times I have been insulting as well. Father, I ask that I might become a creative agent of change in my spouse's life in the future. I commit from this day forward to agape my spouse for the rest of my life. I accept that you have commanded me to do so in Scripture. I will sacrificially love my spouse from this day forward apart from his or her performance. By faith, I will look forward to Your changing my life and my spouse's life where needed through Christ's love. Father, I also commit to return a blessing when my spouse insults me in the future. Allow me to entrust myself to Your Word. In the name of Jesus, Amen.

 THOUGHTS FOR THE ROAD

Complete the week four *Daily Walks* and small group discussion before reading these notes.

LOVE AND BLESSING: GOD'S INSTRUMENTS FOR CHANGE IN MARRIAGE

Sometime after the wedding day, many marriages move from blessing oases to insult battlefields. Many believe fault always rests elsewhere. Arguments are truly vain attempts to try to change a spouse. But, nowhere in Scripture are we encouraged to change other people. Yet, since the fall of man, husbands and wives have specialized in developing new and creative ways of changing their spouse. The subtle variations of these plans can overwhelm even the wisest of marriage counselors.

Only God can change people, and He has ordained only two forces of change in marriage: the active force of love and the reactive force of blessing. Through the application of these principles, God promises that He will change our spouse for us. He might even change our lives as well!

THE ACTIVE FORCE OF LOVE IS GOD'S FIRST AGENT OF CHANGE IN ONENESS

Our culture often defines love in ways that raise false expectations. Couples must settle in their minds what the definition of true love is.

Natural human love is limited as an agent of change in oneness.

The Greek language (used in the original New Testament) specifically defines three words for love.

Eros love is self-oriented.

This word represents a love that is emotional and physical, with emphasis on meeting the desires of the one who seeks love. Although *eros* love was commonly used in Greek literature, it is never mentioned in Scripture. And though man believes it is a valid type of love, the Holy Spirit does not. This love is performance driven and seeks to please only self.

Philos love is friendship.

This love constitutes a significant improvement over *eros* love and involves mutual affection between two people. Mutual concern overrides the mere selfishness of *eros* love. Most Christian marriages are based on *philos* love. Initially, mutual respect and affection draw the couple together. Unfortunately, after several years of marriage, many philos relationships begin to deteriorate into *eros* relationships. As couples focus on each other's performance, they find themselves losing mutual respect. Selfishness and rights can replace tender affection.

Agape love is sacrificial love.

The third word for love, *agape*, is divinely developed and motivated. Apart from God and knowing Scripture, *agape* love would never be humanly possible. *Agape* love is the love Christ constantly refers to in the New Testament. It is the love that will help you to have a faith relationship (Eph. 5:25–29).

God's agape *love is unlimited as an agent of change in marriage.*

Agape love is sacrificial. It is directed by God. Agape is first an issue between God and man, not between two people. It is not based on feelings and circumstances, but rather commitment and a steadfast will.

1. *Agape* love breeds more love and faith by casting out fear (1 John 4:7-11, 18

and Eph. 5:25–33). *Agape* love creates the security of never hearing your spouse say, "I don't love you anymore." When you commit to sacrificially love (*agape*) your spouse for life, both of you are released to renewed strength and hope physically, emotionally, and spiritually.

2. *Agape* love builds respect (John 15:13). The sacrificial nature of agape love tends to build respect for the person giving it.

3. *Agape* love results in the fulfillment of God's biblical promises (1 John 4:19). We cannot personally change our spouse. Only *agape* love—God's love through us—changes people. By an act of your will you can commit to "*agape*" your spouse. Only a love that is unconditional, a love that is independent from your spouse's actions and reactions, will work. God will begin the process of changing your spouse as you *agape* him or her.

THE REACTIVE FORCE OF BLESSING IS GOD'S SECOND INSTRUMENT OF CHANGE IN MARRIAGE.

*E*very person has a capacity to insult others in tough situations, yet God teaches us to react by blessing our spouse, even when wronged, if we want to positively change him/her.

Married couples must understand that their destructive natures threaten oneness.

The Scripture gives many examples of insults and their destructive force. Here are several:

1. Name-calling (Matthew 5:22)

2. Sarcasm and ridicule (Ephesians 5:4)

3. A quarrelsome (nagging) wife (Proverbs 21:9 and 27:15–16)

4. A contentious man (Proverbs 26:21)

5. An unbridled tongue (James 3:5–10)

6. Lying to a spouse (Proverbs 12:22)

7. Insult and abuse in general (Galatians 5:19–21)

Married couples should practice the powerful force of blessing.

An insult is usually the natural human response, while blessing a person requires a godly perspective and a decision of the will. Let us consider several uses of the word "blessing" from Scripture and how they might apply to our marriages.

1. Giving praise to God and your spouse (Luke 1:64; 6:28; 2 Timothy 1:3–6)

2. Giving thanks to God for your spouse and giving thanks to your spouse (Luke 2:28 and Mark 6:41)

3. Calling down God's favor; praying for your spouse (1 Samuel 12:23)

4. Giving benefits or gifts to your spouse (Mark 6:41; Luke 11:13)

5. Seeking the counsel of your spouse (Proverbs 27:9)

6. Giving encouragement to your spouse (Philippians 2:1–4)

HUMAN NATURE CONFLICTS WITH GOD'S CALL TO GIVE A BLESSING.

Because Adam sinned, humankind inherited a self-centered nature that is generally insensitive. This self-centered nature originates ideas and passions that conflict with God's Word and plan for our lives.

1. The perspectives of people and God conflict in many ways. (See chart, right.)

2. God condemns revenge (Romans 12:17–21; 1 Thessalonians 5:15).

FOUR REASONS TO RETURN A BLESSING WHEN YOUR SPOUSE INSULTS YOU

We should respond with blessing because it is God's will as well as the door to personal blessing and God's favor on our life!

1. You will be blessed (1 Peter 3:8–9).

2. You will enjoy life (1 Peter 3:10).

3. God will hear your prayers (1 Peter 3:12a).

4. God is against those who insult or wrong another (1 Peter 3:12b).

MAN'S PERSPECTIVE VERSUS GOD'S PERSPECTIVE

MAN'S PERSPECTIVE (THE WORLD'S SYSTEM)	GOD'S PERSPECTIVE
People are my problem.	"For our struggle is not against flesh and blood, but against the … powers, against the … spiritual forces of wickedness in the heavenly places" (Ephesians 6:12).
Success is the first priority.	"Seek first His kingdom and His righteousness, and all these things will be added to you" (Matthew 6:33).
Hold on to what you've got at all costs or you will lose everything.	"Give, and it will be given to you. They will pour into your lap a good measure—pressed down, shaken together, and running over" (Luke 6:38).
Material possessions will bring more happiness.	"Blessed are those who hunger and thirst for righteousness, for they shall be satisfied" (Matthew 5:6).
Most of my problems are caused by the one in authority.	"Every person is to be in subjection to the governing authorities. For there is no authority except from God, and those which exist are established by God. For rulers are not a cause of fear for good behavior, but for evil" (Romans 13:1, 3).
Love your friends, but get your enemies before they get you.	"But I say to you, love your enemies and pray for those who persecute you" (Matthew 5:44).
If only I had married someone more gifted I would be happier.	"But one and the same Spirit works all these things, distributing to each one individually just as He wills" (1 Corinthians 12:11).
In this life, you've got to take care of Old Number One.	"If anyone wants to be first, he shall be last of all and servant of all" (Mark 9:35).
My mate can't do anything. If only I had married someone God can use.	"I planted, Apollos watered, but God was causing the growth. So then neither the one who plants nor the one who waters is anything, but God who causes the growth" (1 Corinthians 3:6–7).
I'll teach him or her not to cross me.	"Never take your own revenge, beloved, but leave room for the wrath of God, for it is written, 'Vengeance is Mine, I will repay,' says the Lord" (Romans 12:19).
I'm going to the top and I don't care whom I have to step on to get there.	"Humble yourselves under the mighty hand of God, that He may exalt you at the proper time" (1 Peter 5:6).

GIVING A BLESSING, THOUGH DIFFICULT, IS POSSIBLE BY FOLLOWING GOD'S PLAN.

*B*ecause responding with a blessing is difficult, many couples are confused as to how to practically respond to an insult. Fortunately, the Scriptures give clear guidelines on how to render a blessing and how to rid ourselves of the response of insults.

Four steps in responding to insults can be drawn from Christ's example, as described in 1 Peter 2:21–25. When your spouse insults you, you should take the following steps.

1. Remove any sin from your own life (verse 22).

2. Purpose to bless, not insult, the person who hurt you (verse 23a).

3. Commit yourself and your situation to the Lord (verse 23b).

4. Be willing to suffer in order to be reconciled to your offender (verses 24–25).

Note that Christ's blessings did not condone the actions taken against Him.

You can stop the insult cycle in your marriage by starting a blessing cycle.

1. If you follow your natural human instinct, an insult cycle will result.

Entering into a cycle of insults leads eventually to (1) a failure to be one in your marriage, (2) a failure to reflect, reproduce, and reign, and (3) a failure to receive a blessing.

2. If you follow God's Word by faith and respond to your spouse's insult with a blessing, a blessing cycle will follow.

Please review the chart, "The Cycles of Insults and Blessings," shown on the next page. Clearly when you retaliate to an insult with one of your own, more insults come. But when you answer an insult with a blessing, your spouse will become convicted, and further words of blessing make it likely that your spouse will bless you. This results in oneness, an ability to reflect, reproduce, and reign, and receiving a blessing.

The Cycles of Insults and Blessings

INSULT CYCLE

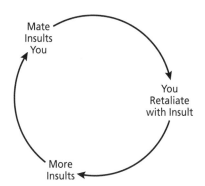

BLESSING CYCLE

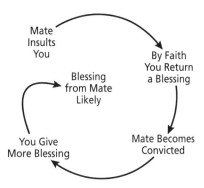

3. The Holy Spirit can enable you to respond in a Christ-like manner.

As you repeatedly bless your spouse when wronged, you will find the result so encouraging that it will become easier over time.

When you exercise agape love as an active force of change in your marriage, and when you react to insult with blessing, you will see God work in your marriage and experience the blessing of a supernatural faith relationship. Remember: Only God can change your spouse, but He often does it through your agape love and by responding with blessing when wronged.

God's Order for

MARITAL ONENESS:

Mutual Love and Respect

Submit to one another out of reverence for Christ.

(EPHESIANS 5:21).

GOD'S ORDER FOR MARITAL ONENESS

Start talking about marital roles based on gender in this culture and you might as well trade in your clothes for a bearskin, grab a club, and label your forehead with "Neanderthal." Needless to say, it's not a popular topic. Yet, God never cared much about man's opinions. He never based His truth on polling numbers. He never makes decisions with the help of focus groups. Therefore, much of His truth about the divine order in marriage has been misunderstood for centuries.

Men hear, "For the husband is the head of the wife" (Ephesians 5:23), and they cheer for joy! A husband interprets this verse to demand a level of performance from his wife. A much sought after queen on her wedding day can quickly turn into a short-order cook, maid, and bedroom servant. After all, "I'm king of the castle," a man states.

Women hear the Apostle Peter say, "be submissive to your own husbands" (1 Peter 3:1), and the first reaction is, "No problem Peter. I'll willingly submit. As long as my husband is attentive, takes out the trash, plays with the children, doesn't turn on the TV when he comes home, and of course, leads in a spiritually sensitive manner …" You fill in the blank. It's natural to think of a wife's response to her husband as conditional, based on his performance, "If my husband acts this way, then I will honor, serve, and love him faithfully."

As you might expect, God calls men and women to a higher plain, a radical perspective, and one that is opposite to man's thinking.

A QUICK LOOK AHEAD

If you want a model for the roles of husband and wife in marriage, you need to go the architect of marriage — God. Unfortunately few topics in Scripture have created as much misunderstanding.

You may have questions in your own mind about how God views gender roles within the confines of the home:

- Did God create men and women equally?
- Did God intend for men and women to have different roles in the family?
- Do men have an advantage over women from God's perspective?

We have come a long way in our journey from *performance* to *faith* in marriage. Accepting by faith God's purpose, provision, power, and instruments of change will definitely move us towards intimacy in our marital relationship. However, blocking our path towards the fifth and final principle for oneness stands a staunch enemy.

When the serpent slithered into the Garden in Genesis 3, the first thing he attacked was the unity of husband and wife. After Adam and Eve had taken their first bite of sin, the family suffered as a recurring casualty throughout the Book of Genesis. The sanctity of marriage stumbled through incest (Noah), role reversal (Abraham and Sarah), and jealousy leading to tag-team child bearing (Jacob, Rachel, and Leah). From the beginning one of Satan's chief goals has been the break up of the family. Once he poisons the root of oneness between husband and wife, his fruit can spread to generations.

1 DAILY WALK, DAY ONE

Make sure you read last week's study notes before starting this section.
Review:

1. How would you describe the differences between *eros*, *philos*, and *agape* love? Why is *agape* love unique and necessary to oneness?

_____

_____

_____

_____

_____

2. From the example that Christ provides for us in 1 Peter 2:21-25, list four steps you might use to respond with a blessing when wronged.

_____

_____

_____

3. Why is it often futile to try to change your spouse? In what ways do you try to change your spouse? Why don't they work?

_____

_____

_____

_____

4. What are the necessary forces God ordained to change our spouse? Have you tried to apply these to your marriage? If so, how?

_____

_____

_____

✦ *Faith Steps* ✦

Remember, these exercises will not be discussed in class.

Part One (Personal)
Spend some time alone with God praying about the following issues:

Admit any failing in the past to love your spouse and to return a blessing when wronged.
Accept your responsibility to love (*agape*) sacrificially, apart from your spouse's performance. Then accept your responsibility, and confess to God any failure to return a blessing instead of an insult when wronged.

Thank God for your new understanding of the following:
•Agape love may allow God to change your spouse.
•Returning a blessing when wronged may not only stop the insult cycle, but may encourage your spouse to change and bless you in return.

By faith, commit to believe God concerning the following issues:

• Commit to love (*agape*) and bless your spouse in the future.
• Commit to suffer momentarily to demonstrate these commitments to your spouse.

Part Two (As a Couple)

Once again, your ability to effectively communicate your new commitments to your spouse is vital. The more you demonstrate and communicate, then, the more God will be able to work in your spouse's life.

Before the date of your next small group, schedule a few minutes alone with your spouse. Your goal at this time should be to verbalize your commitments.

1.   Start your time by discussing your new understanding of the meaning of the word love.

2.   Creatively tell your spouse of your new commitment of love. Assure your spouse that he or she need not ever worry about hearing you say, "I don't love you anymore." Make a commitment to remove the word "divorce" from your vocabulary (Mal. 2:16).

3.   Discuss your new understanding of the principle of returning a blessing when wronged.

4.   Creatively verbalize your commitment to bless your spouse when you are wronged in the future. Encourage your spouse to join you in this faith decision.

Before you begin your second daily journey, read chapter eight and nine in your companion book, Two Becoming One, *by Don and Sally Meredith.*

2 DAILY WALK, DAY TWO

God ordained a plan for roles in marriage. Rather than inhibiting or stifling, these roles were intended to bring blessing and freedom into a marriage. When God ordained distinct roles in the Trinity (1 Corinthians 11:3), He did so for a purpose and it wasn't to make Jesus or the Holy Spirit less than God. In fact they are all equal in essence, but different in role.

Before we look into the dynamic roles of husband and wife, let's examine why God's plan for this relationship is so misunderstood. It started with a serpent's deception using a piece of fruit.

1.   Look up Genesis 3:1-7 and 1 John 2:16. To what human instincts did Satan appeal to when he deceived Adam and Eve?

LUST OF THE EYES, LUST OF THE FLESH PRIDE OF LIFE

2.   What lie did Adam and Eve believe concerning the tree in the middle of the garden?

_____

_____

_____

3. How did Satan's lie compare to God's statements about the tree?

_____

_____

_____

4. Look up Genesis 3:8-14. What were Adam and Eve trying to hide and why? How did sin affect their oneness? Who did Adam ultimately blame?

_____

_____

_____

_____

3 DAILY WALK, DAY THREE

From the Fall in Genesis 3, we see every marriage has fallen into the *performance* trap. When Adam blamed Eve, he pointed to his wife's shortcomings for their problems rather than his own sin. The "blame game" has been played in marriages ever since.

1. Read the verses below about the enemy we face:

For our struggle is not against flesh and blood, but against the rulers, against the powers, against the world forces of this darkness, against the spiritual forces of wickedness in the heavenly places (Ephesians 6:12).

You are of your father the devil, and you want to do the desires of your father. He was a murderer from the beginning, and does not stand in the truth because there is no truth in him. Whenever he speaks a lie, he speaks from his own nature, for he is a liar and the father of lies (John 8:44).

What is Satan's basic nature and how does he use that in marriage?

_____

_____

_____

Why would Satan want you to view your spouse as the problem in your marriage?

_____

_____

_____

2. In light of his deceit in the garden, how does Satan try to deceive husbands and wives when it comes to their roles and God's order in marriage?

_____

_____

_____

_____

3. Why do we often view our marital roles as limitations? (Consider as well the pressures of society and culture.)

_____

_____

_____

 # DAILY WALK, DAY FOUR

While Satan has purposely attacked marriage through deception, the Scriptures outline God's perfect structure for marriage. As we begin to look at the Bible's instruction to husbands and wives, remember: Satan always takes God's good intentions for us and perverts them.

Open up your Bibles and let's start with two key passages: Ephesians 5:21–33 and 1 Peter 3:7.

In our first passage, notice what God says in Ephesians 5:21:

Submit to one another out of reverence for Christ.

Before He commanded the husband to love his wife, or for the wife to respect her husband (Ephesians 5:33), He commanded them both to submit to each other.

Submitting to one another means listening to each other's heart, respecting the other's opinions, honoring each other's thoughts, and serving the other's needs before yours. In addition, notice that in Ephesians 5:18, God commands us to be filled with the Spirit before any of this can occur.

That takes us back to faith principle number three. Without God's power we will not be able to accept God's order in marriage. If a husband or wife is not walking in the Spirit, neither one can be obedient in the process of submitting. Now let's study the different commands to the husband and wife.

Instructions for husbands: *(to be answered by men)*

1. List the commandments given to husbands in Ephesians 5:25–33 and 1 Peter 3:7.

When God tells us to love and submit, He intends only order, blessing, and oneness— not struggle.

_____

_____

_____

2. Husbands are called to love their wives as Christ loves the Church.
How does this practically apply to you?

_____

_____

3. Look up 1 Peter 3:7. What does it mean to live with your wife in an
understanding way?

_____

_____

4. Where do you struggle the most in trying to lead your wife?

_____

_____

NOTE TO HUSBANDS:

The word submit may be defined as "voluntarily placing oneself under another's authority." Husbands, the Bible never tells you to make your wives submit to you. Your responsibility is to love your wife (agape). If you properly love and respect your wife, it will not be hard for her to submit to you. Submission is always the voluntary action of the wife as she understands God's perspective. Remember, the way a husband treats his wife has a major influence on her willingness to submit. In 1 Peter 3:7 (NASB), Peter tells husbands to "understand" their wives and to treat them as the [physically] "weaker vessels." Have you taken the time to be an expert at understanding your wife? The word "vessel" means something very valuable, exquisite in fact. This vessel is "fine china," not everyday pottery that you would treat lightly, but china to be treated with utmost care. Your wife is the very best gift God could give you. If you treat her as fine china, submission will not be an issue in your marriage.

Instructions for wives: *(to be answered by women)*

1. Look up 1 Peter 3:1–6 and Ephesians 5:22-24, 33 and list the commandments
given to wives.

_____

_____

_____

2. Where do you find your greatest struggle in trying to submit to your husband's leadership of the home?

_____

_____

3. List the blessings given to a wife who trusts in God and respects her husband.

_____

_____

_____

[5] DAILY WALK, DAY FIVE

Now that we have examined God's commands to husbands and wives, study the example of Christ's relationship to the Father. It leaves no uncertainty about how to apply the passages that we just reviewed.

1. Look up Luke 22:25-27. How would you define a leader who "lords it over them?"

_____

_____

2. How does Christ describe the second kind of leader in this passage? How many different ways can a husband practice this type of leadership? Think practically here.

_____

_____

_____

3. *For husbands:* If Christ were to ask your wife what type of leader you are in the family, how would she respond? What areas do you think need improvement?

_____

_____

_____

For wives: If Christ were to ask your husband how you submit to his leadership, how would he respond? What areas do you think need improvement?

_____

_____

_____

4. Look up Philippians 2:1-8. How should Christ's example affect our attitudes in marriage?

_____

_____

_____

5. What role in your marriage should a husband's love and a wife's submission play in resolving a difference of opinion?

_____

_____

_____

In week one we learned:

FAITH PRINCIPLE NUMBER **ONE**:

By faith, we must commit ourselves to God's purposes of reflecting His image, reproducing a godly heritage, and reigning in spiritual warfare.

In week two we learned:

FAITH PRINCIPLE NUMBER **TWO**:

By faith, we must receive our spouse from God as His personal provision for our individual needs.

In week three we learned:

FAITH PRINCIPLE NUMBER **THREE**:

By faith, we must daily commit to release the power of the Holy Spirit in our lives.

In week four we learned:

FAITH PRINCIPLE NUMBER **FOUR**:

By faith, we must submit to the only active and reactive biblical forces for change in marriage: agape love and blessing.

THEREFORE, GOD'S **FIFTH** FAITH-BASED PRINCIPLE FOR ONENESS IS:

By faith, we must seek

God's wisdom concerning our responsibilities

of mutual love and respect.

⇾ *Apply the Principle* ⇽

Think about a marriage you admire. It could be parents, grandparents, family friends, or a neighbor. It needs to be someone whom you have had time to examine.

1. What made their marriage stand out?

_____

_____

_____

2. How did they emulate the principles we studied this week: love and submission?

_____

_____

_____

3. In light of our study, what is one practical way you could change your actions toward your spouse?

_____

_____

_____

Commit to sharing your action in a creative way to your spouse this week.

A QUICK LOOK BACK

There is no 50/50 relationship in marriage. God's plan is always 100/100. In order for a marriage to work, both husband and wife need to submit their own lives to God and then to the roles God ordained from creation. Wives, trust God and be submissive to your husbands; husbands love your wives as Christ loved the Church. If one neglects his or her role, it's like rowing a boat with one oar. It will go nowhere. However, that doesn't mean either party has the right to abandon the ship. Ironically, when we accept by faith the position of God's order for marriage, then we will experience whatever every person desires but rarely finds: true intimacy, true oneness.

❧ BECOMING ONE PRAYER

FOR HUSBANDS: *Heavenly Father, thank You for Your Word and how it gives me wisdom concerning my role as a husband. Please forgive me for my past failure to love my wife as Christ loved the Church. Protect me from Satan's deceit in the future. I commit to avoid being a "lording" husband and ask for the humility to truly serve my wife's needs. Allow me to love and cherish her sacrificially as my own body and help me to encourage and motivate her. By faith, I am going to trust You to sanctify her while causing her to be more internally and externally beautiful, as well as making her all that you created her to be. In the name of Jesus, Amen.*

❧ BECOMING ONE PRAYER

FOR WIVES: *Heavenly Father, thank You for Your Word and how it gives me wisdom concerning my role as a wife. Please forgive me for my past failure to demonstrate a submissive and respectful spirit to my husband. Protect me from Satan's deceit in the future. Give me the faith to humbly serve my husband's needs and allow me to demonstrate a loving and respectful attitude toward him. By faith, I am going to trust You to work in his life while You take the responsibility for my needs. Thank You that I can be fearless as I trust You. In the name of Jesus, Amen.*

Complete the week five *Daily Walks* and small group discussion before reading these notes.

LOVE AND RESPECT: GOD'S TOOLS FOR MARITAL ONENESS

*I*n this day and age when you talk about the roles of husbands and wives in a marriage relationship, you get a very strong response.

Questions like this arise:

- Does the husband have the advantage?
- Is the wife limited by submission?

Few other issues have more potential to destroy oneness and impede God's purposes for marriage.

Satan has been lying to couples since the Garden of Eden. Because many couples do not know Scripture, they believe Satan's lies. But from God's perspective, fulfilling His marital roles gives us joy and hope.

SATAN'S LIES AND MAN'S SIN

*B*efore the fall of man, husband and wife fulfilled marital responsibilities. In the Garden, God instructed and blessed Adam and Eve. Exposed in every way, Adam and Eve trusted fully in God's purposes for their lives.

Since the Fall, husbands and wives have struggled with their responsibilities. Sin shifted the eyes of Adam and Eve from God to themselves, resulting in a preoccupation with self. Adam and Eve lost the experience of oneness.

Shortly after they began the "Blame Game." Adam blamed Eve and failed to take responsibility for his sin. He then blamed God. Eve blamed the serpent. Selfish pride replaced oneness and order.

Adam and Eve believed Satan's lies and consequently sinned. In his deceit in the Garden of Eden, we see how Satan appeals to our selfishness by making us believe that God's provision is a limitation. Once we believe Satan's lies, our natural human nature leads us to sin.

When God originally instructed us to love and submit, His design was for us to experience relationships, to meet our needs, and to equip us to reflect, reproduce, and reign. A person viewing life from God's perspective knows that the one who loves has no advantage over the one who responds. But our flesh resents the difference. Satan is out to destroy our oneness.

God knew that there would be neither satisfying relationships nor oneness without love and submission. Yet God had always intended good. Only through our mutual love and submission can God meet our aloneness needs. Agape relationships exist only when mutual love and respect exist.

HUSBANDS AND WIVES MUST RESIST SATAN'S DECEIT BY HOLDING FAST TO GOD'S PERSPECTIVE.

God's command to the man to love his wife and the wife's command to submit to, or respect, her husband make this clear (Ephesians 5:22–33; 1 Peter 3:1–7). The key to maintaining God's order for marital oneness is to show love, submission, and respect toward each other.

The biblical commands show that God created neither spouse with an advantage.

Ephesians 5:22–33 and 1 Peter 3:1–7 contain commands that leave little doubt about the responsibilities of the husband and wife. Both passages command absolute love and submission. Each also offers a number of exciting promises that become the hope and motivation to carry out the commands.

- Love must be sacrificial (husbands, Ephesians 5:25).
- Submission is to be "as to the Lord" (wives, Ephesians 5:22-24; 1 Peter 3:1–2).

Let's examine the promises attached to the commands to love and submit.

It becomes apparent that God created neither spouse with an advantage.

God makes it easier to love and submit by drawing our eyes away from the **commands** and putting them on the **promises** that will be fulfilled when we love and submit by faith.

- A husband's love frees the wife to become godly in her character (Ephesians 5:26).
- A husband's love frees the wife to become characterized by an outward attractiveness and an inner joy as well as becoming all that God created her to be (Ephesians 5:27).

- A husband's sensitivity to his wife frees his prayer life (1 Peter 3:7).
- A wife's submission silences the protests of a husband (1 Peter 2:15).
- A wife's respectful behavior can move her husband toward God (1 Peter 3:1).
- A wife who trusts God more than human devices will be very precious to God (1 Peter 3:3–4).
- A woman who puts her trust in God, not her husband, will have no fear (1 Peter 3:5–6).

There is biblical wisdom in showing love and submission in marriage.

God tells husbands and wives to love and submit for the following reasons:
- It allows us to accomplish His purposes for marriage: reflecting, reproducing, and reigning.
- God is the Author and the Guarantor of our relational needs; therefore, He protects the one who loves and the one who submits.
- Since God is a God of order, He made mankind to exist in counterparts and within a structure (1 Corinthians 11:3, 11–12).

Love and submission can be further explained by New Testament practice and example.

In the New Testament we see that respect for each other is essential. Jesus Christ Himself made this clear:

But you are not to be like [the world's powerbrokers]. Instead, the greatest among you should be like the youngest, and the one who rules like the one who serves. For who is greater, the one who is at the table or the one who serves? Is it not the one who is at the table? But I am among you as one who serves (LUKE 22:26–27).

Genesis 2:18 best captures a wife's hope of blessing her husband and reflecting the image of God: "A helper suitable for him." An excellent yet brief description of a suitable helper appears in Titus 2:3: "reverent in [her] behavior" (see also verse 4–5). When a wife views life from God's perspective, she is not as vulnerable to the attacks of Satan because she knows God's Word and entrusts herself to Him. Her trust in God leads her to unite her strength to His to create a godly family.

Only God's perspective allows a wife to bless her husband. If you are a wife, your husband is alone and he desperately needs a companion, a helper, a completer, a friend!

Ultimate wisdom regards love and submission as blessings to bestow. Christ's trust of God the Father allowed Him to view love and submission as the greatest blessings in all eternity. Philippians 2:1-11 illustrates for us the attitude of Christ, "do nothing out of selfish ambition or vain conceit, but in humility consider others better than yourselves."

Humility is a key to achieving God's goal for your marriage – oneness. Humility is not emotional cowering, but a mark of strength and trust in God. Without humility, there is no encouragement, love, fellowship, affection, or compassion.

CHRIST IS THE MODEL FOR LOVE AND SUBMISSION.

Submission and servant leadership are normal traits of the committed disciple of Christ. We are first and foremost submitted to God and His direction for our lives. Secondly, we are called to love others before ourselves.

And being found in appearance as a man, he humbled himself and became obedient to death— even death on a cross! Therefore God exalted him to the highest place and gave him the name that is above every name (PHILIPPIANS 2:8–9).

Our model of servant leadership and submission is found in Jesus Christ. Although He is one with the Father and part of the Godhead, He has always chosen to submit Himself to the will and purposes of His Father. As He was selfless in His servanthood to God the Father, we too must draw on His model of love and His model of submission. Both His love and His submission brought Him to the cross. And then God vindicated Him through the resurrection.

Submission in marriage operates on three levels:

1. Both the husband and wife in submission to the lordship of Jesus Christ (Romans 12:1)

2. Mutual submission to one and other out of "reverence for Christ" (Ephesians 5:21)

3. The wife's willing submission to her loving husband (Ephesians 5:22-5:24)

In other words, we are brothers and sisters in Christ before we are husbands and wives. Therefore, our marriage is always a part of something larger and greater than itself – Christ and His relationship to the church.

The responsibilities of the one in authority are sacrificial love, care, concern, provision and direction – always in obedience to God Himself. The responsibilities of the one in submission are to be joyful and willing to do God's will – always trusting God to work both in and through the designated authority. The limits to submission are always obeying God before, or in spite of, those in authority over us. God is always to be our first priority.

Above all else, a husband should be a servant. Sadly, many Christian husbands choose to define their role as the "superior" one because of Satan's deceit and their own self-centered viewpoint. Remember, Christ did not reflect a love that was haughty or willful (Luke 22:26–27). He was not prideful.

Jesus continues to model humble service. The one who died for the Church now prays for her and provides for her future. He encourages her submission to His Father's will, but He never lords Himself over the Church. Christ, who is Lord, does not condone any form of lording. He teaches us that leaders are to be servants.

SO HOW DO THE ROLES OF LOVE AND SUBMISSION WORK IN MARRIAGE?

If loving each other unconditionally is your daily practice, only on rare occasions should the issue of submission come into play. One rule of thumb is to communicate, especially when it comes to major decisions. We'll repeat this for emphasis: *communicate on every major decision.*

There are such things as minor mutual agreement matters. These might include tastes in music, food, arts, media, quiet time styles, sleeping and arising, etc. Major issues might include: choosing a home church, having children, how many children to have, making a career change, moving to a new location, purchasing major items, making financial investments, paying bills, and of course intimacy issues.

Biblical submission arises whenever a major issue cannot be mutually agreed upon or whenever a crisis throws a major mutual agreement up for grabs. For instance, if the husband's company wants to move him to another city with a pay raise and the wife does not want to make that move. Or the wife feels like they should start a family, but the husband does not. What do you do in situations like these?

First, prayerfully ask some questions:
- Are we both willing to trust God to speak and work through our spouse?
- Have we sufficiently discussed the issue in order to know all the factors involved?
- Is it really a submission issue?
- Are we too emotionally involved to see the larger issue?
- Are there other unresolved issues clouding this decision – hurt feelings, personal neglect, a root of bitterness, a lack of forgiveness, past abuse in making decisions, etc.?
- Are we committed to glorifying God?
- Are we committed to following godly priorities?
- Are we committed to Christ-like servanthood?
- Is there anything in the Word of God that we are not following?
- Have we sought godly counsel?
- Have we spent sufficient time in prayer and/or fasting?
- Have we asked friends or family to pray with us about this decision?
- As the husband, have I taken into account my wife, my children—their feelings and direction on this issue? Am I loving them properly in order for them to pray adequately and for my wife to feel free to trust God in my decision?
- As the wife, am I willing to trust that the Lord has our family and me in His hands? Am I willing to trust and rely on my husband's judgment when my own feelings are not the same as his?

When these questions have been asked and answered, and a decision deadline is approaching, but you are still in disagreement, then the issues of love and submission come into play. Under the loving leadership of the husband, the wife will joyfully submit to him and ultimately to Christ and then they both can watch God work for their benefit. These are rare occasions for the husband and wife, but God usually tests couples on their willingness to either lovingly lead or willingly submit.

HUSBANDS AND WIVES MUST COMMIT TO GOD'S PERSPECTIVE BY FAITH.

God did not create love and submission as limitations, but as principles for healthy relationships and oneness – a return to the Garden. In addition, biblical love and submission lead to the ultimate glorification of Jesus Christ: the accomplishment of God's purposes in the universe.

The choice is yours. Will you commit to God's perspective of love and submission, or will you perpetuate the lie Satan started in the Garden?

ONENESS... OUR PART

Acting by Faith:

Marital Trials
(Week Six)

Romance
and Sexual Fulfillment
(Week Seven)

Communication and
Resolving Conflict
(Week Eight)

WEEK SIX:

Marital
TRIALS

Consider it all joy, my brethren, when you encounter

various trials, knowing that the testing

of your faith produces endurance, and let endurance

have its perfect result, that you

may be perfect and complete, lacking in nothing

(JAMES 1:2-4, NASB).

THE JOURNEY THROUGH MARITAL TRIALS

The day was April 13, 1970. About 3,000 miles from the earth, a red light started beeping. Three men realized this wasn't a false alarm on the *Apollo 13* console. Suddenly, "perilous" was an understatement. They couldn't just turn back and go home. The ejector seat was not an option. Captain Jim Lovell uttered the well-known words, "Houston, we have a problem."

Every journey encounters problems from the mundane to life-altering experiences. You feel them when you embark on an eight-hour odyssey to grandma's and right as you pull out of the driveway, your toddler asks, "Are we there yet?"

You realize them when you're hiking in the mountains and the weatherman's "sure-fire forecast" of "not a cloud in the sky today" did not include the huge black ones massing above your head.

You realize them when someone drops a letter on your desk with the words "company downsizing."

In those situations, you can always turn the car around or hike back to shelter. But in marriage, when we encounter problems, much like the astronauts in *Apollo 13*, we can't just turn back. There's no ejector seat.

"God, we have a problem."

For the past five weeks we have started down the journey towards intimacy. We've accepted by faith God's principles for oneness. It's one thing to accept God's principles, it's another thing to act on them. The true test of oneness will come when we encounter struggles in our marriage. Our first temptation will be to chuck the principles and run back to what's comfortable—blame, anger, apathy, treating our spouse as the problem, in a word, *performance*.

In the next three weeks we will examine three areas with which every marriage will struggle: marital trials, sexual expression, and communication. How we apply God's faith principles for oneness will determine if struggles in those areas lead us to greater intimacy or to a desire to push the ejector seat button.

A QUICK LOOK AHEAD

Imagine sailing with your spouse in the Caribbean (remember seasickness doesn't exist in a daydream!). Sea gulls dot the barren sky, the water is clear as blue glass, and the gentle breeze fills the sails. Suddenly black clouds race towards the boat, the glass-like water shatters with ten-foot swells, and the winds rip through the canvas. Then, if the weather wasn't bad enough, you and your spouse start arguing over who is to blame for the storm!

Sound foolish? You would think that arguing would be the most counterproductive way to fight the storm. Yet when storms buffet the home in the form of infertility, debt, rebellious teenagers, job loss, in-laws, etc., most couples respond by attacking each other rather than weathering the squall together.

Sailors expect storms. It's not if they happen, it's when. We should expect to face trials in marriage. Instead of dividing us, storms should unite us against the struggle.

- How do you handle storms in your marriage?
- Are you quick to blame your spouse for trials or do you band together?
- Is it possible that trials can lead us to a greater depth of intimacy?

This week we will learn to identify trials and prepare for their impact in our marriages. We will then examine how God uses the storms of life to make our marriages stronger and move us toward oneness.

 DAILY WALK, DAY ONE

Make sure you read last week's study notes before starting this section.
Review:

1. Explain how Satan has distorted God's intentions for love and submission in marriage. How have these distortions caused stress in your marriage?

_____

_____

_____

_____

2. How does the world's perspective of roles differ from God's perspective? Does this create tension in your marriage? Why or why not?

_____

_____

_____

3. What commitments have you put in place to help you love your wife or submit to your husband?

_____

_____

4. Define how love and submission function when making a major decision.

_____

_____

_____

✦ *Faith Steps* ✦

Remember, these exercises will not be discussed in class.

Part One (Personal)

As we learned last week, we will not move our marriage from performance to faith without accepting God's order for marital oneness. Husbands are to love their wives as Christ loved the Church. Wives are to submit to their husbands. Let's recommit to this order through personal prayer and mutual promises.

Take some time today to pray about how you can exhibit the qualities of love and submission in your marriage.

1. Start by confessing any failures in the following areas:
- Any subtle doubting of God's fairness concerning love or submission.
- Any hurt you may have caused your spouse by your past failure to love or submit.
- Any willful rebellion you may have demonstrated in your love or submission to your spouse because of pride.

2. Commit to believe God concerning the following issues:
- Love and submission are God's creation order for oneness in relationships.
- Love and submission have nothing to do with advantage or inequality.
- Satan is our enemy who deceives us into seeing our spouse as a limitation to our personal fulfillment.
- We should entrust ourselves to God and His promises. Then with humility, we should love and submit to our spouse completely.

Part Two (As a Couple)

1. It's vital that we communicate our commitment to love and submit to our spouse regarding love and submission. Creatively complete the answers to the following statements:

In the past, I have struggled at times with God's command to love or to submit to you because …

_____

_____

_____

I would like to ask your forgiveness for …

_____

_____

_____

In the future, I will show you my love or submission through …

_____

_____

_____

_____

2. Take your spouse out on a date before the next small group meeting. Verbalize your commitments by reading your responses affectionately to each other. Make a covenant together with the Lord regarding your new commitments to each other.

2 DAILY WALK, DAY TWO

The better you are at anticipating trials, the more growth you will experience in your faith.

During the past five weeks, we have learned principles that, when applied by faith, will produce a *faith-based relationship*. Now we are going to grasp some practical tools for becoming one—starting with trials.

When trials hit, our first temptation will be to abandon the faith principles and return to what is familiar, comfortable, and easy—*performance*. We will look to blame rather than bless, pout rather than pray, and lash out rather than love.

So before we look at trials common to every marriage, we need to make sure the faith principles for oneness are ingrained in our hearts and minds.

1. From weeks 1-5, list below the five faith based principles for oneness.

_____

_____

_____

_____

_____

_____

_____

2. Which one(s) will, if applied, greatly help you in your marriage right now? Why?

_____

_____

_____

_____

3. How would you define the difference between a marriage based on performance and one based on faith?

_____

_____

3 DAILY WALK, DAY THREE

Often when Christian couples seek marital counsel, the counselor soon learns they are not really having marital problems. Instead, the couple is experiencing a tough trial in life. Because they have neither properly recognized the trial nor responded wisely, the couple has transferred the pain of the trial to their marriage.

Trials are inevitable in the Christian life and marriage as well. Let's define trials and what we can expect as a result of them.

1. Look up the word "trial" in a dictionary and write the definition below.

_____

_____

_____

Before you begin your third daily journey, read chapter sixteen in your companion book, Two Becoming One, by Don and Sally Meredith.

2. Read 1 Peter 4:12 below:

Dear friends, do not be surprised at the painful trial you are suffering, as though something strange were happening to you.

How does this verse impact your view of trials in marriage?

_____

_____

_____

3. Look up 1 Peter 4:12-19, and list your observations of how we are to respond to trials.

_____

_____

_____

4. Are you and your spouse going through a trial right now? If so, explain.

_____

_____

_____

_____

Trials not only develop endurance but maturity. The phrase "lacking in nothing" means equipped with every resource. Endurance, complete maturity, and being equipped with every resource— that's quite a promise!

[4] DAILY WALK, DAY FOUR

Now that we have defined trials and realized that they will be a part of our marriage, let's examine God's purposes for trials and how we are expected to respond to them.

1. Read the passage below:

Blessed is the man who perseveres under trial, because when he has stood the test, he will receive the crown of life that God has promised to those who love him (JAMES 1:12).

What is the reward for those who have suffered in a trial?

_____

_____

_____

2. Study the verses below that describe life's trials, and summarize what our responses to those trials should be in the right column.

RESPONDING TO TRIALS

VERSES ON LIFE'S TRIALS	OUR RESPONSE TO TRIALS
JAMES 1:2-4 (NASB) *The testing of your faith produces endurance.*	
HEBREWS 12:2-3 *Fix our eyes on Jesus... who...endured the cross.*	
2 CORINTHIANS 4:7-10 *not crushed...not in despair... not abandoned ...not destroyed.*	
2 CORINTHIANS 4:16-18 *Therefore we do not lose heart.*	
PSALM 119:71-72 *It was good for me to be afflicted.*	
PSALM 119:75-76 *In faithfulness you have afflicted me.*	
2 CORINTHIANS 1:4-5 *[God] comforts us in all our troubles, so that we comfort those in any trouble.*	

3. Read 2 Corinthians 12:7-10. While trials ultimately end, a "thorn in the flesh" may not. According to Paul, what was the purpose of his thorn?

_____

_____

4. Do you have a perceived "thorn" in your life? If so, explain how it affects your marriage.

_____

_____

_____

5 DAILY WALK, DAY FIVE

As we go through trials, we often experience various symptoms from the pressure or stress that is involved. Many of these symptoms can be seen in Job's life in Scripture. Knowing the symptoms can often help us to recognize when we're facing a trial.

1. Read each of the following verses from the Book of Job and identify the symptom or symptoms mentioned. Use your own words to describe the symptoms. The first two have been completed as examples.

SYMPTOMS RESULTING FROM TRIALS

BIBLE VERSE	SYMPTOM
JOB 3:24	*sighing, loss of appetite, groaning*
JOB 3:26	*restless, anxious, lack of sleep*
JOB 4:5	
JOB 6:26	
JOB 7:4	
JOB 7:11	
JOB 7:20	
JOB 16:16	
JOB 17:7	
JOB 23:3-4	
JOB 30:16	

2. Have you experienced any of these symptoms when you were in a "trial" period? If so, which ones?

_____

_____

_____

3. Read and summarize Job's attitude concerning trials in the space provided.

    Job 1:20

    _____

    Job 2:10

    _____

    Job 5:18

    _____

    Job 13:15

    _____

4. The Bible contains many characters who endured various trials (for a great listing, read chapter 11 in the book of Hebrews). Select one or two of your favorite biblical characters and list the types of trials they faced. How well did they cope with the trial? How could they have responded better?

_____

_____

_____

_____

✧ *Personal Application* ✦

Trials come in various shapes and sizes. Whether it's financial, parental, or physical, our intimacy in marriage can be compromised depending on how we handle the trial. We will move back towards *performance* if we blame our spouse or expect our spouse to fix it during the trial. We will move to *faith* if we see the trial as an opportunity for growth and greater intimacy.

1. What have been some of the hardest trials you faced?

_____

_____

2. How did those trials drive you apart from your spouse? Or how did the trial deepen your relationship?

_____

_____

3. In hindsight, what spiritual lessons did you learn from those trials?

_____

_____

A QUICK LOOK BACK

Are you expecting trials in your marriage? More importantly, are you moving through them by *faith* or by *performance*? God has indicated that we will all experience trials. If we see them as an opportunity for growth, God will move our marriages to deeper levels of intimacy.

BECOMING ONE PRAYER

Heavenly Father, I confess to You that I have resented and feared trials in the past. I have many times refused to recognize them as coming from You and instead have blamed those around me. Please forgive me for my unbelief. In the future, I commit to examine every painful event, circumstance, or action as if it were a trial. I commit to join with my spouse to view the trial from Your perspective. Give me the strength to persevere in trials. Give me joy at the thought of becoming more mature and complete from the trial. Thank you that I can join in Christ's suffering and, ultimately, in His exaltation. Allow my faith to comfort my children and family. Cause me to renew my mind with Your Word during my trials. Thank You for Your faithfulness. In the name of Jesus, Amen.

THOUGHTS FOR THE ROAD

Complete the week six *Daily Walks* and small group discussion before reading these notes.

TRIALS: GOD'S TOOL FOR GROWTH IN MARRIAGE

When the storms of life wreak havoc in your marriage, do you and your spouse blame each other, or work together to find a solution?

Every journey encounters problems and few journeys are as problem-filled as marriage. Trials such as job loss, death in the family, and parenting can take their toll on spouse. However, depending on your response, trials can either draw you together as a couple, or move you farther apart.

Married couples at times seek counseling because of pain and stress caused by the trials one or both spouses are experiencing. Often they improperly blame the pain of the trial on their relationship and wrongly conclude, "We have a marriage problem." Nothing defeats marital oneness more than failure to recognize and support one's spouse during a trial.

In the Bible, we learn that the way one responds to trials will often determine one's success in life and marriage.

EXPECT TRIALS TO BE A NORMAL PART OF YOUR MARRIAGE.

We must learn to anticipate and recognize trials.

As Christians, we often equate trials with failure and thus set out to avoid them. Yet God has a totally different perspective of trials. To God, trials are a blessing that bring growth and maturity. Obviously, God's perspective is totally opposite from our natural, limited human outlook.

Trials can be defined as periods of adversity.

The New Webster's Dictionary and Thesaurus of the English Language calls

trials "adversity, suffering, troubles" and, significantly, "a test of faith." We can expect "various trials" in our lives, according to James 1:2. Trials are periods of adversity, and vary in nature and often come when we least expect them.

Every Christian marriage will encounter trials.

When speaking of life's trials, Peter said, "Dear friends, do not be surprised at the painful trial you are suffering, as though something strange were happening to you" (1 Peter 4:12). Why is it we always seem surprised or taken off guard by trials? We say, "Why me?" "Why now?" Peter states that Christians should expect trials! And for Christian couples, such adversity provides yet another opportunity to experience oneness in marriage.

God is moving us toward more intimacy – both with Him and with each other. He knows that trials are often the method that produces the greater good.

Remember that God is conforming us to the image of Jesus Christ, and trials develop dependence on Him and strengthen our faith in Him. Potentially trials can change husbands and wives for the better. God sometimes uses trials as a method of discipline for His children (see Hebrews 12:4-11).

Our Christian forefathers encountered trials.

It is impossible for Christians to become Christ-like without trials, "To this you were called, because Christ suffered for you, leaving you an example, that you should follow in his steps" (1 Peter 2:21). Just as Christ could not have reached His goal without trials and suffering, we cannot reach ours.

Historically, this has always been true. Consider this brief list of biblical characters and the trials they suffered.

- Abraham and Sarah: Infertility, moving, loss of culture and family, and the test of sacrificing their son.
- Joseph: Death of mother, a dysfunctional family, hurt and rejection by his brothers, unjustly put in prison, loss of family, and loss of own culture.
- Moses: Loss of his culture, murder, nomadic lifestyle, working with rebellious people, and experiencing an unfulfilled dream by not seeing the Promised Land.
- Job: Loss of his children and material possessions, health problems, and loss of his wife's respect.
- David: Adultery with Bathsheba resulting in pregnancy, the loss of a child, murder, and rebellious children.
- Mary and Joseph: Crisis pregnancy and ridicule, slander, moving, and the death of their firstborn son, Jesus.
- Paul: Persecuted, shipwrecked, imprisoned, and a nagging thorn in the flesh.

COUPLES MUST EXPECT TRIALS TO AID THEM, DESPITE MOMENTARY SUFFERING.

Our focus should not be on the suffering aspect of trials, but on the benefits and blessings God promises.

Trials help couples mature by developing their dependence on God.

James understood this maturation process well. He states, "the testing of your faith develops perseverance.

Perseverance must finish its work so that you may be mature and complete, not lacking anything" (James 1:3–4).

Consider this: The very trial that you hate the most may be the necessary tool that God uses to perfect your worst flaws, or your spouse's. Indeed, the circumstance may be a trial to you because of your flaws. God is moving you towards maturity.

"Fixing our eyes on Jesus, the author and perfecter of faith, who for the joy set before Him endured the cross, despising the shame, and has sat down at the right hand of the throne of God. For consider Him who has endured such hostility by sinners against Himself, so that you will not grow weary and lose heart"(Hebrews 12:2-3).

Christ focused not on the horrible pain of the cross, but on the joy of salvation that resulted for us in eternity. Therefore, He was able to endure His momentary suffering. We too must focus on the joy of maturity and positive spiritual change. Trials cause us to fix our eyes on Christ, thereby overriding our human sinful inclination to rely on ourselves.

Trials teach couples that momentary suffering leads to long-term blessing.

Through Scripture, God continually communicates the promise of blessing to Christians who persevere through trials. Strength to endure these trials comes from memorizing and meditating on the promises of Scripture (for example: 2 Corinthians 4:17; James 1:12). We can pray back to Him these Scriptures and realize that "this trial, too, will pass" and that God will use it to teach us vital life lessons.

Trials teach couples to trust God's character and commandments.

When couples trust God's perspective concerning trials and fix their eyes on Him, they begin to see God more clearly. God's faithfulness and Word begin to take on new meaning. The book of Psalms encourages us: "I know, O Lord, that your laws are righteous, and in faithfulness you have afflicted me. May your unfailing love be my comfort, according to your promise to your servant" (Psalm 119: 75–76; see also verses 67 and 71).

Through trials, God is able to demonstrate Himself to us. His Word becomes reality. His faithfulness becomes our hope. His unfailing love serves as our comfort.

Trials teach couples that true power comes only from God.

Today, our culture teaches us that power comes within each person. With positive reinforcement or an "attitude adjustment," the world teaches we can do the impossible. But Scripture teaches us that trials should draw us to His power, not ours: "in jars of clay to show that this all-surpassing power is from God and not from us" (2 Corinthians 4:7). Trials prove our deep need for dependence on God's power. They allow us to experience God's faithfulness and the great resources He provides.

Trials teach couples not to exalt themselves.

Pride and self-centeredness are great enemies of oneness in marriage. God uses trials in our lives to rebuke these natural weaknesses in our character.

Read the riveting account of Paul's life where God used a struggle to humble him (2 Corinthians 12:6–9). Paul exalted Christ's power instead of his own. The more we trust ourselves, the more we will struggle with pride and self-centeredness. Similarly, God used trials to humble the nation of Israel (Deuteronomy 8:2).

Humility releases God's power to sustain us through our trials. He often brings a trial into our lives to ensure that we trust Him to meet our needs instead of counting on ourselves.

Trials teach couples to be compassionate toward each other as well as others.

During painful trials such as infertility, job loss, and family deaths, Christians can find particular comfort in the marriage relationship. Thus God works through trials to stimulate loving support from one another, resulting in a stronger marriage (2 Corinthians 1:4–5).

As you and your spouse suffer through trials, each of you will gradually see the importance of providing comfort to the other. Over time, your mutual compassion for each other will grow.

MARITAL ONENESS IS DEPENDENT ON COUPLES QUICKLY RECOGNIZING TRIALS AND PROPERLY RESPONDING TO THEM.

Three failures concerning trials have plagued Christian marriages over the years:
1. The failure to anticipate and recognize trials.
2. The failure to understand the purpose of trials.
3. The failure to support one another during difficult trials.

Couples must be quick to recognize trials.

1. The first priority in recognizing trials is to identify their symptoms.

Trials produce a variety of symptoms that act as warning signals of difficulties. The Book of Job provides an excellent list of symptoms with which with you might identify. If the cause does not become readily apparent, obtaining outside counsel may be wise.

2. Some trials are common to marriage.

Trials come in many forms and from many sources. The young and less-experienced couple will most likely be surprised at the great variety of trials that they may face.

When identifying a trial in your life, consider the common trials shown in the chart, "Typical Marital Trials." If you believe you recognize a trial you are facing, discuss it with your spouse. Then together, develop a strategy for standing together as you deal with the trial.

3. Couples must realize the importance of agreeing together concerning their trials.

The primary benefit of quickly recognizing trials is being able to support one another instead of blaming each other or your marriage. Disagreement concerning the trial can result in a lack of support for one another, making oneness impossible. Without oneness, the pain of the trial will be greatly increased.

It is important not to underestimate the power of praying together in the face of trials, since prayer usually leads to oneness and agreement on your coping strategy (see God's promise related to prayer and trials in James 1:5-8).

TYPICAL MARITAL TRIALS

MARRIAGE
Lost commitment
Sexual conflict
Adultery
Poor communication
In-law conflicts
Abuse (physical/
    spiritual)
Rejection of spouse—
    body, personality,
    intellectual,
    spiritual, vocational,
    as a parent, or
    health issues
Elderly parents
Ex-spouse problems

FINANCIAL
Debt
Foreclosure
Bankruptcy
Mortgage
Taxes
Budget
Savings
Giving
Spending
Spouse
    irresponsibility

CHILDREN
Pregnancy
Death of a child
Discipline problems
Academic problems
Learning disability
Self-image problem
Two or more children
    under age six
Stepchildren
Leaving home
Health/handicapped
Lack of spouse support
Teens/puberty

GENERAL
Death in the family
Death of a friend
Alcoholism
Drug abuse
Retirement
Education
Legal problems
Vacations
Holidays

PERSONAL
Friend
Work
Schedule
Priorities

HEALTH
Illness
Injury
Diet
Weight
Exercise
Hysterectomy
Back
Heart
Cancer
Ulcer
Sexual dysfunction
Infertility

VOCATION
Readjustment
Job change
Fired
Lost interest
Conflict
Relocation

CHANGE
Financial
Residential
School
Church
Social/Isolation
Sleep habits/
    Self image

Once identified, couples must respond to the trial with God's perspective.

1. Determine if you brought the trial into your life or if God allowed it in your life.

If you determine that you brought the trial into your life through sin, irresponsible behavior, or a bad decision, confess it to God. After your confession, take the appropriate steps to resolve it. Be sure to seek forgiveness from others when appropriate. If you need counsel, look for a good biblical counselor to assist you. The sooner you confess your sin, the sooner the consequences of the sin will subside. Dealing with personal sin and failure quickly brings negative consequences under control sooner (see James 1:13-20).

If you have not brought the trial into your life, assume God allowed it from His loving hand for your benefit and His glory. Begin to apply the perspectives taught in the Scripture concerning trials. As you apply these perspectives, begin to thank the Lord for the trial. You will be blessed for your faith.

Review the other possible sources of trials: (1) Other people—The world that we live in can be a source of trials; sometimes these trials are beyond our control, and other times they are avoidable; (2) Satan—Satan and his forces can cause trials in our lives (for example, Job 1:6–12); yet Scripture assures us that we have ultimate power over Satan; and (3) God— He may allow a trial in our lives in order to test and refine our faith in Him.

No matter what the source of a trial, God's solution is always the same. We must trust in God's faithfulness and His sovereignty over our lives.

2. Determine to respond in faith to the trial.

When the full force of a trial hits, we can become discouraged and blame others, even God, or we can respond with God's perspective. Our natural instinct is to lose hope or blame. Yet if we have renewed our minds with Scripture, we have the choice of responding in faith, choosing to override our human instinct.

FOUR STEPS FOR DEALING WITH TRIALS

Step One: Anytime prolonged tension confronts the marriage, the couple should begin to evaluate if a new trial has begun.

Step Two: Commit yourselves to the Lord by seeking His perspective on the trial. Remember that the divine perspective will include the following:
- God knows what He is doing in our lives. He is sovereign and wise.
- God knows that trials are good for us, leading us toward maturity, as well as a deeper walk with Christ.
- The trial God takes us through may, in fact, be saving or preserving our lives and marriage.
- God sees our trial as a blessing, not a curse.
- God takes us through trials so that we might better understand Him, ourselves, and others.

Step Three: Evaluate your actions and the lessons God wants to teach you. Seek for-giveness and restitution when necessary.

Step Four: Develop a creative strategy to support one another while working through the trial. If the trial is avoidable, take immediate corrective action. Commit to the Lord that you will move through this trial by *faith*.

Once you are over the trial, examine how well you handled it with your spouse. Discuss how it may have been handled in a better fashion. This analysis will help prepare you for the next trial.

Trials are seldom pleasant, but the anguish that comes with them can be mitigated by knowing that God will use them to perfect you. At all costs, do not allow trials to drive you and your spouse apart. If the trial persists or the pain becomes too much, seek the wisdom of a Christian counselor or church leader. Jesus says, "Come to Me, all who are weary and heavy-laden, and I will give you rest" (Matthew 11:28).

WEEK SEVEN:

ROMANCE
and Sexual Fulfillment

My beloved is mine, and I am his...

his desire is for me

(SONG OF SOLOMON 2:16; 7:10, NASB).

MEMORY VERSE (HUSBANDS)

Rejoice in the wife of your youth...

may you ever be captivated by her love

(PROVERBS 5:18-19).

ROMANCE AND SEXUAL FULFILLMENT

*I*n our culture, sex sells everything from cars to carbonated drinks, from bran flakes to boats. Our society promotes sexuality as more fantasy than reality. If someone wanted to write a book about sex in marriage, the title might be *Great Expectations*.

Unfortunately reality is quick to shatter expectations. The bedroom in our homes rarely matches the bedrooms on television or the movies. Marriage counselors all over America consistently report that couples struggle with sex.

Such a chasm between expectations and reality leaves many couples disillusioned and disappointed. So where do you turn? At home, the conversation feels awkward, the church is silent, and the world doesn't offer any reality-based solutions.

Where are you in your sexual relationship? Fulfilled or frustrated? Are your expectations meeting reality? When you have honest questions, where do you turn for practical answers?

The answer may surprise you …

A QUICK LOOK AHEAD

It's impossible to talk about performance in your marriage without opening up Pandora's box of romance and sex.

Few areas in our marriage lug as much baggage as sex. Expectations are at an all time high. Husbands expect their wives to be Victoria's Secret models. Wives expect Cassanova to sweep her off her feet. With such great expectations, both ultimately end up being disappointed. At the same time, any meaningful conversation on the subject gets pushed aside by dishes, kids, work, and church events. It's easier just to pull the covers over the exasperation.

Not this week. This week we will alay our misconceptions about sex.

- The Bible doesn't have anything to say about sex ... does it?
- Why doesn't my spouse feel the same way I do about sex?
- Should sex always be spontaneous?
- Why are men and women so different?

Then, after a few eternal tips from the Creator of sex, we'll turn our great expectations into a better reality.

Note: After discussing the day one journey in your small group, you will split into separate groups of men and women to discuss the rest of your daily journeys.

 DAILY WALK, DAY ONE

Make sure you read last week's study notes before starting this section.
Review:

1. In light of 1 Peter 4:12, how do you think God wants you to handle trials differently as a couple? Give specific examples.

_____

_____

_____

_____

✦ Faith Steps ✦

Remember, these exercises will not be discussed in class unless otherwise noted.

1. Review the chart "Typical Marital Trials" in last week's notes; then, on the chart, draw an "H" (husband) or "W" (wife) over any symptoms that have arisen out of those trials.

2. Now that you have identified your trials and symptoms, prioritize them below. List the first trial as the one most pressing at this moment. List your personal trials and symptoms, then your spouse's, and finally your trials as a couple. There will probably be overlap in some of your responses.

——— TRIALS AND SYMPTOMS ———

MY TOP 3 SYMPTOMS

1:_____

2:_____

3 _____

MY TOP 3 TRIALS

1:_____

2:_____

3 _____

MY SPOUSE'S TOP 3 SYMPTOMS

1:_____

2:_____

3 _____

MY SPOUSE'S TOP 3 TRIALS

1:_____

2:_____

3 _____

OUR TOP 3 SYMPTOMS
AS A COUPLE

1:_____

2:_____

3 _____

OUR TOP 3 TRIALS
AS A COUPLE:

1:_____

2:_____

3 _____

---

3. After identifying your trials, look back to the "Four Steps for Dealing with Trials" from last week's notes, and develop a strategy for persevering and supporting one another in these trials.

4. Individually complete the statements below, one for each trial you are facing as a couple:

a. When I think about how you could best support me on this trial, I need for you to:

_____

_____

b. When I think about how I could best support you on this trial, I feel I need for me to:

_____

_____

Before you begin your second daily journey, read chapter twelve and thirteen in your companion book, Two Becoming One, *by Don and Sally Meredith.*

2 DAILY WALK, DAY TWO

Today we begin our study of the sexual relationship in marriage. Being aware of God's attitude and wisdom is important to a change in our perspective. We are confident you will discover that *God is positive, even enthusiastic about the sexual relationship in marriage.*

First, let's talk frankly about our struggles and successes with sex and romance.

TRUTH 1 – SEXUALITY IS GOD'S CREATION.

1. Look up Genesis 1:27 and 2:24-25. According to these verses, who created sex?

_____

2. How does your answer compare with the perception of our culture? Explain.

_____

_____

TRUTH 2 – PHYSICAL LOVE IS FOR PROCREATION AND PLEASURE.

3. Read the verse below, and circle key words and/or phrases that reveal God's enthusiasm for sexuality.

Put me like a seal over your heart, like a seal on your arm. For love is as strong as death, jealousy is as severe as Sheol; its flashes are flashes of fire, the very flame of the Lord (SONG OF SOLOMON 8:6).

The purposes of sexual love go beyond just procreation. Consider the strong words the Holy Spirit uses to describe sexual love: death, flashes of fire, blessed, rejoice, satisfy, and captivated (read Proverbs 5:18-19).

Feelings and romance usually are the result of a healthy relationship, not its cause.

4. What does describing sex as "the very flame of the Lord" mean?

_____

_____

5. Look up Psalm 127:3. We've seen that pleasure is one of God's purposes for sex. What is another part of God's plan for our union?

_____

TRUTH 3 – PHYSICAL LOVE IS A PICTURE OF CHRIST AND THE CHURCH.

6. Look up Ephesians 5:31-32, and discuss how this picture of Christ and the Church relates to marriage, including sexual intimacy.

_____

_____

_____

3 DAILY WALK, DAY THREE

Most couples will need to reprogram their minds because of faulty church, parental, or societal teachings on sex. The Bible communicates numerous truths in this area that we will consider over the next three days. These insights will help us move from performance driven physical intimacy to a *faith-based view of sexuality and romance.*

TRUTH 4 – PHYSICAL LOVE DEMANDS A TIME PRIORITY.

1. Look up Deuteronomy 24:5. The phrase "bring happiness" in Deuteronomy 24:5 could be interpreted "learn to fulfill sexually." This Jewish practice tells us a lot about God's priority for the sexual union. What could have been God's purpose in limiting a husband's outside responsibilities in the first year of marriage?

_____

_____

2. Why is it important for the wife to know that her husband is available to her and is learning to meet her needs?

_____

_____

3. Look up Song of Solomon 7:11–12. Why is it important to "get away" occasionally to replenish your lovemaking abilities?

_____

_____

TRUTH 5 - PHYSICAL LOVE REQUIRES TRANSFER OF BODY OWNERSHIP.

4. Look up 1 Corinthians 7:3–4. What is God's point in these verses? Why is the point important for experiencing "oneness" in marriage?

_____

_____

5. What stumbling blocks do you have with this guideline, if any? How do you think these faith principles could help solve this?

_____

_____

_____

4 DAILY WALK, DAY FOUR

TRUTH 6 - PHYSICAL LOVE IS TO BE PASSIONATE AND CREATIVE.

1. Look up Song of Solomon 4:16; 5:1; 6:13. In these verses Solomon and his bride use "garden," "fruits," and "fragrance" as metaphors for physical intimacy. How would you describe their emotions and level of excitement?

_____

_____

_____

2. How did Solomon's wife entice him sexually (Song of Solomon 2:6; 4:16)?

_____

_____

TRUTH 7 - SCRIPTURE ADVOCATES VERBAL COMMUNICATION DURING SEXUAL LOVE.

3. Look up Song of Solomon 5:10–16; 7:1-9. What is occurring between Solomon and his wife in these passages?

_____

_____

4. What can you learn about the differences between men and women in these passages? (Notice where each starts and stops in the description of the other.)

_____

_____

_____

[5] DAILY WALK, DAY FIVE

TRUTH 8 - PHYSICAL LOVE SHOULD OCCUR REGULARLY.

1. Look up 1 Corinthians 7:5. Becoming "one flesh" is not automatic. It takes more than just time priority. How important is consistent sexual contact between husbands and wives?

_____

_____

2. What exceptions are mentioned in the preceding verse?

_____

_____

TRUTH 9 - PHYSICAL LOVE IS MORE THAN PHYSICAL.

3. Look up Song of Solomon 5:2–8. We should not focus on the physical aspects of sexuality to the neglect of the emotional, spiritual, and intellectual needs of our spouse. Summarize below the Shulamite's eagerness to respond to Solomon after initially rejecting him? What do we learn from this?

_____

_____

4. Now summarize how Solomon responded to his wife (6:4–10). What can we learn from this interchange?

_____

_____

_____

TRUTH 10 - PHYSICAL LOVE GIVES COMFORT AND HEALING.

5. Look up 2 Samuel 12:24. Sexual love is a manifestation of what God calls "one flesh," a oneness that goes beyond just the sexual act. How could the sexual union bring comfort to a hurting heart?

_____

_____

TRUTH 11 - THE PARENTS TRANSFER ATTITUDES ABOUT SEXUAL PURITY TO THEIR CHILDREN.

6. Look up Song of Solomon 8:8-9. The younger sister is described as either a "wall" (steadfast against temptation) or a "door" (easily swung into temptation). How does the text describe how the brothers will protect her?

_____

_____

Pray that your kids will be "walls." Unfortunately most teenagers know more about the details of driving a car than they do the intricacies of the sexual experience. We should be motivated by Scripture to explain clearly, with sensitivity and tenderness, the temptations and traps of sexual intimacy before marriage.

✦ *Personal Application* ✦

This week we want to make an exception. **Go ahead and read the notes for this chapter. Pay special attention to the last few pages on creating "naked and unashamed" experiences.** Then come back and finish this section.

Begin now to establish a habit of making time for just the two of you.

Often when someone hears about "planning" such experiences in a marriage, a *performance-based relationship* will say:
    "Sex should be totally spontaneous."
    "My spouse should intuitively know what I need."
    "Prayer totally disrupts the romance of the moment."

But when a couple acts by faith on God's truths about sexuality and romance, they will experience fulfillment in their physical and emotional oneness.
    When you fail to plan, you plan to fail. So to help you achieve sexual fulfillment in your marriage, take these practical and creative steps:

Step One – Pull out your calendars.

Step Two – Carve out time in the next three months.

1. Schedule several 24 hour "naked and unashamed" experiences.

2. Schedule several 2 hour "naked and unashamed" experiences .

Step Three – Plan the experiences.

Vary who is responsible for the experiences. Sometimes it should be the husband, the wife, and then both of you plan them together. Also be in diligent prayer for the experiences.

Warning: With kids, church, work, and keeping a house this can easily become just another check-off on your to-do list. Make sure you have realistic expectations for the 24-hour and 2-hour "naked and unashamed" experiences. Habits generally take time to establish, but once they are established, they become a natural flow of life. These times should revitalize and refresh you on the journey from performance to faith in your marriage.

Step Four – Evaluate and plan again.

Take time to evaluate what worked, what you liked, what you would do again, and what you would change. Then take out the calendars and plan the next few months. If you intentionally make a habit of carving out time for romance and sexuality, you will notice a vast improvement in the depth of your intimacy.

A QUICK LOOK BACK

Many couples weather the storm of a frustrating sexual relationship without making adjustments. It's simply easier to bury the bitterness rather than exert the energy to change. But we've learned that God has much to teach us in this area. Rather than being a source of struggle, romance and sexuality can be a source of strength and intimacy in your marriage.

❤2 BECOMING ONE PRAYER

Heavenly Father, thank You for creating my sexuality. I confess to You that I have not always honored You by my sexual actions or attitudes. Please forgive me. Lord, may Your Holy Spirit open our marriage to Your maximum sexual experience. I now understand Your pleasure in my sexual union with my spouse. Lord, give my spouse a sensitive understanding of my fears and concerns sexually and me of his (or hers). Allow us to creatively approach the future with Your Word in mind. Open me to counsel if I hit obstacles that discourage my spouse. Bless us with the ability to "drink our fill" sexually so we may honor You. In the name of Jesus, Amen.

These notes will help you with your application section in this chapter.

SEXUAL EXPRESSION:
GOD'S GIFT FOR ONENESS IN MARRIAGE

So, where are you in your sexual relationship? Fulfilled or frustrated? If you are like most couples, you are probably somewhere on that spectrum. With the pressures from culture and media, often our expectations about romance and sexual expression rarely meet reality.

Sexual issues frequently create problems in marriage. There are three primary reasons for this:

1. A wrong view of human sexuality. Christians are being incorrectly programmed by the culture to view sex as a non-relational, automatic experience.

2. Selfish attitudes regarding sex. Christians struggle sexually because of their self-centered natures. Left unchecked, this can destroy God's purpose for the sexual relationship.

3. Lack of biblical guidance regarding sex. Historically, biblical teachers have been hesitant to share Scripture's excitement and wisdom concerning the sexual relationship. Given this void of biblical truth, Christians simply follow the world's perspective on sexuality.

Nevertheless, God is totally committed to the sexual relationship in marriage. In Scripture we see that God calls sexual love in marriage "the very flame of the Lord" (Song of Solomon 8:6). The sexual relationship is a unique characteristic of marriage, and sex was designed to be both beautiful and exciting.

GOD CREATED SEX AND IS
COMMITTED TO HUMAN SEXUALITY.

As Christians, our first priority must be discovering what Scripture says concerning sexual love. God's truth will help you maximize your experience of sexual love in marriage.

The sexual relationship is given tremendous value in Scripture.

The following biblical truths reflect God's view of sexuality, as well as our hope for sexual healing throughout our culture.

- Sexuality is God's creation.
- Sexual love is for procreation and pleasure.
- Sexual love is a picture of the union of Christ and the Church.
- Sexual love demands a time priority.
- Sexual love requires transfer of body ownership.
- Sexual love is to be passionate and creative.

- Scripture advocates verbal communication during sexual love.
- Sexual love should occur regularly.
- Sexual love is more than physical.
- Sexual love gives comfort and healing.
- Sexual attitudes of parents are transferred to children.

God identifies sexuality as a distinctive of marriage and oneness.

God has established sex as a primary ingredient of oneness in marriage. "They shall become one flesh" (Genesis 2:24) describes the essence of oneness in marriage. "One flesh" carries a sexual meaning. In Deuteronomy 24:5, the sexual relationship is given first priority over work and war.

The gift of sex in marriage is a picture of the spiritual union of Christ and the Church.

God uses sex to picture the union of Christ and His Church in Ephesians 5:31–32: "For this reason a man will leave his father and mother and be united to his wife, and the two will become one flesh. This is a profound mystery—but I am talking about Christ and the church."

We use much the same marriage terminology when describing our relationship with Christ. Our earthly intimacy with our spouse is a picture of our spiritual relationship with Christ. We are the "bride," He is the "Groom."

Christ offers grace to us through salvation. The physical union in marriage is a means of offering grace to one another. When I give my body to my spouse willingly, I am giving out of a heart of grace.

GOD CREATED HUSBANDS AND WIVES WITH UNIQUE SEXUAL DIFFERENCES.

Some wonder why God made sex so tough to discuss. With sexual intimacy serving as such a profound image of our spiritual relationship with Christ, Satan does his best to demoralize, marginalize, and demean this intimate act. In addition, conversation requires us to serve one another's different approaches and needs in sex.

The doors to sexual satisfaction are different for husbands and wives.

Song of Solomon 5:10–16, 7:1–9 show the different approaches of men and women toward sex. In Song of Solomon 5, the wife focuses on his face— she is relational. In Song of Solomon 7, the husband focuses generally on her midsection – he is physical.

Let's look at some of the differences between men and women. As we look at the doorways to healthy sexuality, we must generalize a bit. If you do not fit exactly into these generalizations, don't be frustrated—God is bigger than these generalizations.

The door to sexual satisfaction for a man tends to be physical (sight and touch; see Job 31:1).

Men tend to be stimulated by sight and they generally think about sex more often then women. Research indicates that young men under age thirty think of sex up to ten times an hour. A husband needs a wife who is both sensitive and open to stimulating him through sight and touch.

The door to sexual satisfaction for wives tends to be emotional and relational.

When Ann Landers took a poll of 90,000 women, 64,000 said a "warm hug" sufficiently met their needs physically. The door to sexual satisfaction tends to be very different for women than men. Women find that sex works as part of a holistic experience with their husbands. Their husband's relational commitment to them during the 24 hours prior to the sexual experience often means as much to them as the act of sex itself.

A wife needs assurances of her partner's love, such as a hug, a pat, a compliment, or an "I love you." A woman will respond well to a man who actively listens and exhibits understanding of her life and needs.

To sum up, generally, husbands are looking for a woman who is a passionate lover while wives are looking for a sensitive friend. Remember that God created your sexuality and that the best sexual relationships occur when each partner puts the other's needs above his or her own. This is true Christ-like servanthood. Also, remember that these are generalizations—you and your spouse may be different.

Despite their differences, husbands and wives both need the sexual union.

Consider the following ways that both husbands and wives need sexual unity.

1. In their physical oneness, a couple reflects the purposes of God.

In our first chapter we talked about the necessity of accepting God's purposes for marriage. Two of them are emulated by the sexual relationship—an opportunity to reproduce children and reflect His image together.

2. Husbands and wives are healthier if they experience regular sexual expression. Medical research indicates that regular sexual activity enriches both spouses physically.

3. The self-confidence of the husband and wife prospers when their romantic life prospers. As you spend time romancing and cherishing your spouse, your sexual intimacy and enjoyment will grow as well.

4. Enthusiasm for marriage is fostered by sexual unity. Couples who experience full sexual fulfillment enjoy times just as a couple, whether trips together or just a weekend at home alone. Taking time to love is a choice that leads to sexual fulfillment and excitement.

Remember, it is up to each couple to decide how often they have sexual relations. As Solomon wrote, "Eat, O friends, and drink; drink your fill, O lovers" (Song of Solomon 5:1). Whatever you decide together is what is right for you.

5. A couple's sexual excitement positively impacts the whole family.

Few things encourage a child more than mom and dad sneaking a hug and kiss. Conversely, the lack of love between parents can be devastating. How can a wife reflect the fullness of her feminine nature to her daughter without truly loving dad? In like manner, a son will have difficulty defining love correctly if he does not see dad really loving mom. Families prosper better when mom and dad experience a fulfilling sexual life.

HUSBANDS, DEMONSTRATE COMPASSION AND SENSITIVITY TO YOUR WIFE'S PHYSICAL NEEDS.

*I*f a husband wants his wife to be excited sexually, then he must satisfy her emotional and relational needs. Since many men are generally less emotional, husbands must become "detectives" and uncover the issues that block their wives' sense of emotional well-being.

Protect your wife's emotional and sexual freedom.

Emotional stress can become sexual scar tissue that blocks your wife from experiencing sexual fulfillment. For example, hurt, fear, resentment, and anger are emotions that often block sexual satisfaction in women. The issues that cause these emotions must be removed before a sense of emotional well-being can be reestablished in your wife. Remember these ten suggestions for protecting your wife's sexual freedom:

- Emotional investments such as saying "I love you" and showing a deep marital commitment are necessary for sexual satisfaction.

- Poor communication will block sexual openness.

- Emotional pain and hurt caused by unconfessed sin needs to be dealt with before experiencing physical intimacy.

- Failure to view your spouse's body and sexual involvement positively will damage your spouse.

- Especially early in marriage, some sexual expressions can embarrass a spouse.

- Lack of absolute privacy can eliminate the possibility of emotional freedom.

- Schedule crunches diminish sexual expression.

- Physical pain can be a problem at times.

- Physical or emotional hurt will hamper sexual freedom.

- Past sexual or substance abuse should be handled with counseling.

HUSBANDS AND WIVES SHOULD ENJOY THEIR SEXUAL FREEDOM.

Couples often ask, "What can we do to revitalize our sexual experience?" These last two sections are devoted to answering this question.

Communicate—Husbands and wives must be honest about hidden sexual feelings and actions.

What we say and what we think may not be the same. For instance, a wife might say, "I do not feel well right now; do you mind if we don't tonight?" Her husband may think that his wife is feeling physically sick at that moment. Yet, what she may have meant was "I have felt fat all day and the last thing I feel like doing is exposing my body right now." Or, "You haven't been communicating properly with me, and now you want sex! No way!" No wonder couples struggle. It is hard enough to deal properly with the known issues, let alone those that remain hidden.

Consider the following examples of hidden feelings, desires, and actions:

Refuse to substitute your sexual expression with pornography, fantasies, or masturbation.

These things not only hinder oneness in marriage, they also injure the relationship.

Each spouse must be honest with himself or herself and the Lord concerning sexual substitutes. After confessing them to the Lord, share them with your spouse. (The spouse to whom you confessed should not be tempted to judge you.) The couple should then work out a plan to correct the problem by working together to serve one another. Seek help from a counselor if any of these behaviors have become addictive. Help is available.

Your body is not a device for manipulation.

Sometimes husbands and wives make unhealthy sexual bargains. Hidden forms of dishonesty and manipulation are harmful and wrong. Subconsciously saying, "I will punish you sexually for doing that" is wrong and manipulative. God took that right away from us when He gave ownership of each spouse's body to the other (see 1 Corinthians 7:1-5). Therefore, search your own heart to detect guilt. If you are guilty, confess it to God and your spouse. By faith, reassure your spouse of your commitment to not do so in the future.

Refuse to punish for past failures—seek to forgive.

Some couples have a difficult time forgiving and forgetting, and may carry a grudge for years. From God's perspective, few things are worse than failing to forgive, especially in the light of His gracious forgiveness of us.

Stop punishing your spouse for a past failure. However, if there has been a history of adultery or pornography, the guilty party needs continual

> From God's perspective, few things are worse than failing to forgive, especially in the light of His gracious forgiveness of us.

accountability in this area, preferably from a Christian counselor or mentor.

Recognize potential sexual dysfunction.

Sexual dysfunction—an inability to respond sexually or to have sexual interest—can occur in marriage for many reasons. Some forms of dysfunction are physical, some emotional, and others are spiritual. Here are several physical and emotional causes to consider: (1) premature ejaculation or erection problems, (2) sexual pain, (3) drug or alcohol abuse (past or present), (4) past sexual abuse, (5) history of sexual fear and anxiety, (6) history of extreme sexual focus (affairs, pornography, etc.), (7) history of extreme guilt, and (8) some prescribed medicines for depression.

If any of these issues are present in your marriage, seek counsel or medical information.

Couples should focus on total sexual encounters instead of simply on sexual intercourse.

Sexual relations in marriage typically consist of fifteen to twenty minutes and primarily involve intercourse. Lasting sexual excitement is almost impossible in that context. The focus must be on your spouse's total physical person. For both wife and husband, longer encounters that eventually culminate in intercourse satisfy both spouses' needs for romance and endearment.

Certainly there are times when only brief sexual encounters are possible, but in the long run, if couples hope to be one sexually, they must focus their sexual relationship on "holistic" encounters. Holistic encounters, also called "naked and unashamed" experiences, meet the emotional, spiritual, and physical needs of one another.

EACH COUPLE NEEDS "NAKED AND UNASHAMED" EXPERIENCES.

What is a "naked and unashamed" experience?

This unique experience is a one to two hour sexual encounter that has five progressive elements.
• Advance preparation
• Relaxation, communication, and prayer
• Sexual tension and foreplay
• Intercourse/special desires
• Communication (a proper finish)

A "naked and unashamed" experience brings several benefits to a couple's sexual expression.

A naked and unashamed experience provides a couple with:

• Adequate time to experience romance
• Adequate opportunity and time for building sexual tension, which makes for more complete physical responses later
• Ample time to meet the emotional and relational needs of the wife
• An opportunity to communicate spiritually and emotionally
• An opportunity to characterize themselves as "desirable" and "in love"

Ideally, each couple should attempt to have one "naked and unashamed" experience a week. In addition, each couple should plan several twenty-four-hour outings in a year. Certainly this will not be easy, but it will be worth the effort, even if you are only half-successful.

Plan a 24-hour encounter.

A naked and unashamed encounter has the same elements whether the event spans twenty-four hours or two hours. As we consider the common elements, we also will focus on the timeline, beginning with a 24-hour encounter.

Although it is not always easy to take a full day away, it is vital to your oneness. Couples typically succeed here by forming a bond with other couples who have children. These couples commit to keep one another's children while each couple takes a night out.

Communication and planning are key. Determine what a perfect twenty-four hour experience might be for each of you. After that, schedule the details.

Activities prior to the two-hour sexual encounter are next on the schedule. Here is where your mutual planning pays off. Whatever the activities your spouse and you have scheduled for the rest of this special day together, enjoy them. Relaxation, communication, and prayer come next. When the two-hour experience arrives during the 24-hour schedule, the following elements should be included:

1. Begin by relaxing, perhaps with a hot shower or bubble bath together or with a brief nap together. One of you may even need some time alone.

2. Positive communication and prayer are the next order of emotional

freedom. Hurts and concerns must be positively addressed before emotional freedom can follow. Consider these issues in your communication, possibly during a relaxing dinner:
*   Encourage each other and renew faith commitments of love.
*   Catch up on where your spouse is at this point in time.
*   Take time for confession, recommitment, and prayer.

3. During the prior communication period, it would be good for the couple to prepare for their sexual encounter. Ask your spouse what would excite him or her. Husbands make sure to talk with your wife. Enjoy your closeness during conversation. After prayer, begin to open up more. with proper lotions, lighting, and music work great. During this period each spouse should describe in detail something special they would like for their spouse to do sexually during foreplay—no surprises that might frustrate the other.

4. Next, sexual tension and foreplay will open the couple to sexual arousal. While we need not be overly explicit here, couples must understand their need to participate in foreplay, which would include loving touches and kisses. Your conversation during the communication period and after prayer will help lead you into foreplay that is pleasing and delightful to your spouse.

5. Next, move toward completion. While sexual union is not always necessary, it does provide the couple a special sense of oneness. Each spouse often will request some special release sexually, and this is both acceptable

and a loving response. Do not finish until both agree that each feels complete and fulfilled.

6. Finally, have a proper finish. In the twenty-four-hour experience, there is still much to complete on the schedule. Communicate, pray, and tie up the loose ends of picking up children, etc … together.

In conclusion, you can see how the sexual relationship between a husband and wife is vital. It can either be rewarding or discouraging. Remember, when communication and romance focus on marital oneness, even our sex lives, which were created for God's purposes, can bring glory to Him.

Recommended Reading:
- *Intimate Issues*, by Linda Dillow and Lorraine Pintus
- *The Gift of Sex*, by Clifford and Joyce Penner
- *The Act of Marriage*, by Tim and Beverly LaHaye
- *Intended for Pleasure*, by Ed Wheat

WEEK EIGHT:

COMMUNICATION
and Resolving Conflict

Do not let any unwholesome talk

come out of your mouths,

but only what is helpful for building others up

according to their needs,

that it may benefit those who listen

(EPHESIANS 4:29).

COMMUNICATION AND RESOLVING CONFLICT

*H*and grenades or land mines.

We are usually one or the other when it comes to dealing with conflict in marriage. When conflict arises with our spouse (notice the "when," not "if"), we either hurl insults or hide feelings and hope it goes away. Some of us are quick to toss our anger, bitterness, and pain right back at our spouse when a conflict surfaces. Others of us avoid conflict at all costs. We end up burying our hurt until our spouse or even our kids inadvertently detonate the pain.

If you are married as two hand grenades, explosions are probably often, but quick, leaving scars on your souls.

If you are married as two land mines, explosions are rare, but huge, leaving craters in your hearts.

If you are married as a hand grenade and a land mine, watch out, you never know when the explosions will come and they inflict all kinds of damage.

Which one are you?

Communication in marriage should be a major source of blessing, not a battlefield of bitterness where the casualty is our intimacy. If conflict is an expected part of our marriage, how can we create a model of communication that deals with the issues without inflicting more pain?

DAILY WALK, DAY ONE

Make sure you read last week's study notes before starting this section.
Review:

1. What does the Bible teach about sexuality as an expression of oneness in marriage?

_____

_____

_____

_____

_____

✦ *Faith Steps* ✦

Remember, these exercises will not be discussed in class unless otherwise noted.
These practical steps will help us establish a realistic view of your sex life as it currently exists; identify areas in which you are successful, and provide a plan for

how you can improve in sexual expression and romance. Honesty and transparency will be the key to experiencing physical oneness.

Part One (To be completed individually)

1. In response to each of the statements listed in the chart below, circle the number that best characterizes you. Use this scale:

> 1= never, 2= rarely, 3= once in a while, 4= sometimes,
> 5= often, 6= most of the time, 7= always

2. Repeat the exercise, drawing an "X" through the number that best describes the way you think your spouse would appraise you.

EVALUATION OF OUR SEXUAL RELATIONSHIP

Anticipation of sex	1	2	3	4	5	6	7
Natural desire for sex	1	2	3	4	5	6	7
Spouse's interest in my needs	1	2	3	4	5	6	7
Communication concerning sex	1	2	3	4	5	6	7
Effort toward foreplay and lovemaking as a couple	1	2	3	4	5	6	7
Gentleness and tenderness during lovemaking	1	2	3	4	5	6	7
Creativity before and during lovemaking	1	2	3	4	5	6	7
Attention to my spouse's satisfaction during lovemaking	1	2	3	4	5	6	7
Time priority committed to lovemaking	1	2	3	4	5	6	7
Spouse's appreciation of my body	1	2	3	4	5	6	7
Desire to improve our lovemaking	1	2	3	4	5	6	7

Part Two (Personal)
   Complete the following sentences, as if you were speaking to your spouse. (Again, this assignment is to be completed alone, not as a couple.)

1. When I consider your greatest need sexually, I feel you need for me to ...

_____

_____

2. When I consider my greatest need sexually, I feel you need to …

_____

_____

3. Considering these different sexual needs, I feel they could both be met by …

_____

_____

Part Three (As a Couple)

1. Briefly trace the history of your sexual excitement in your marriage. Changes are normal in marriage. Note the reasons for any changes.

_____

_____

_____

_____

2. List and then discuss both your fears and the things that motivate you sexually. If you have thoughts about how to alleviate your fears, mention them.

_____

_____

_____

3. List and discuss any attitudes that either you or your spouse have about your bodies that might hinder your sexual relationship (refer to 1 Corinthians 7:3–5; Song of Solomon 5:1–16; 7:1–9). Be as positive in your statements as you can.

_____

_____

4. What behavior or actions do you consider romantic? Take enough time to be complete in your answer and share it with your spouse.

_____

_____

_____

_____

Part Four (As a Couple)

The purpose of this section is to discuss each other's feelings, attitudes, and thoughts on this subject and to encourage one another. Work on this section together. This exercise will require approximately twenty minutes.

1. Share and discuss as a couple the work you completed in parts one and two. Be sure to share your thoughts with an attitude of understanding, sympathy, and forgiveness. Don't be judgmental or put your spouse down.

2. Schedule a whole day and night within the next month when the two of you can get away together for a special time of communication and intimacy.

[2] DAILY WALK, DAY TWO

Finish the remaining chapters (10,11, 14 & 15) in your companion book, Two Becoming One, *by Don and Sally Meredith.*

While the subject of communication is woven throughout your companion book, *Two Becoming One*, we felt a week of study from God's Word on the subject was vital for you and your spouse.

The key element that Scripture commonly refers to concerning communication is the "human spirit," a supernatural entity that is created by God at conception. Genesis 2:7 describes God's original creation of the human spirit: "The Lord God formed the man from the dust of the ground, and breathed into his nostrils the breath of life, and the man became a living being." The Hebrew word translated "breath of life" is the Hebrew word for human spirit. Thus, body plus spirit equals a living soul.

By far the most common usage of the word spirit in the Bible refers to a person's mood, pervading disposition, or frame of mind. Nothing affects communication more than these three elements. The first thing Scripture tells us to do concerning communication is to check our human spirit, mood, or disposition. Is our spirit positive or negative? Does it encourage or discourage communication?

1. Look up Malachi 2:13–16.
   Husbands are instructed to guard themselves in their spirits. Since the context here is marriage, what part does the human attitude play in marital communication? How can a positive or negative attitude affect communication with our spouse?

_____

_____

_____

_____

_____

2. The following verses contain *positive* examples of the human spirit. List the attribute and explain why you think that quality is important to good communication. The first reference has been completed as an example.

POSITIVE EXAMPLES OF THE HUMAN SPIRIT

SCRIPTURE REFERENCE	TERM/PHRASE	HOW THE QUALITY AIDS GOOD COMMUNICATION
1 Corinthians 16:18	*"refreshing spirit"*	It uplifts and encourages me.
Psalm 51:10		
Matthew 26:41		
Luke 1:47		
Acts 18:25; Romans 12:11		
Galatians 6:1		
Philippians 1:27; 2:2		
1 Peter 1:13; 4:7		

3. The following verses contain negative examples of the human spirit. List the attribute and explain how you think that quality negatively impacts communication.

NEGATIVE EXAMPLES OF THE HUMAN SPIRIT

SCRIPTURE REFERENCE	TERM/PHRASE	HOW THE QUALITY HINDERS GOOD COMMUNICATION
Numbers 5:14	*"jealousy, suspicious nature"*	Jealousy, accusing tones
Genesis 4:6-8		
Exodus 6:9		
Daniel 2:1		

4. Think back to the last "miscommunication" you had with your spouse. Forget the issue for a moment. What was your demeanor? Your attitude? How did your underlying "spirit" affect the conversation?

_____

_____

_____

Romance will die without communi- cation.

3 DAILY WALK, DAY THREE

Another factor that affects communication is each spouse's will. Are you walking in the power of the Holy Spirit, or is your "old self" in control?

1. Look up Ephesians 4:26-31. How do you think removing bitterness, rage, "along with every form of malice" would specifically affect communication with your spouse? How can you effectively remove these attitudes? Why would God want us to deal with anger quickly?

HONEST CONVERSATION STOPPERS. AS MUCH AS WE ARE ABLE w/HOLY SPIRIT "ONLY SUCH AS BUILDING UP THAT FIT THE OCCASSION THAT IT MAY GIVE GRACE. LEST A ROOT OF BITTERNESS SPRING UP.

2. Read the verses below and relate how forgiveness and compassion relate to good communication.

   Then Peter came to Jesus and asked, "Lord, how many times shall I forgive my brother when he sins against me? Up to seven times?" Jesus answered, "I tell you, not seven times, but seventy times seven" (MATTHEW 18:21-22, NASB).

   Bear with each other and forgive whatever grievances you may have against one another. Forgive as the Lord forgave you (COLOSSIANS 3:13).

   Be kind and compassionate to one another, forgiving each other, just as in Christ God forgave you (EPHESIANS 4:32).

   _____

   _____

   _____

3. God calls us to be peacemakers in our own home (Romans 12:18). Why is this crucial to good communication?

   _____

   _____

   _____

4. God calls us to persevere in tough times in our communication with our spouse. Why is "not giving up" an important aspect of good communication? (Matthew 5:44; James 1:12).

   _____

   _____

   _____

[4] DAILY WALK, DAY FOUR

Communication is a two-way street. We need to speak and listen. But too often, our communication in marriage turns into a traffic jam where we speak too fast and slam the brakes on our ears. Today, we will learn about two keys of effective communication: heartfelt listening and speaking the truth in love.

You will notice in the next two exercises that after each verse there is a space. Write down what the verse has to say about listening or speaking the truth in love. Then give a positive or negative example of how this verse was or was not applied in your life. The first verse has been completed as an example.

SCRIPTURAL TRUTHS ABOUT LISTENING

SCRIPTURE REFERENCE	PRINCIPLE AND EXAMPLE FROM MY LIFE
James 1:19-20	Good hearing leads to God's righteousness as well as constraining anger. Personal example: our financial problems last August.
James 1:22	
Proverbs 10:19	
Proverbs 13:3	
Proverbs 13:10	
Proverbs 13:18b	

SCRIPTURAL TRUTHS ABOUT SPEAKING THE TRUTH IN LOVE

SCRIPTURE REFERENCE	PRINCIPLE AND EXAMPLE FROM MY LIFE
Ephesians 4:25	We should be truthful with each other because we are one in Christ and love each other. Personal example: I didn't tell the truth about how much I spent on clothing/electronics.
1 Timothy 1:5	
Proverbs 14:29	
Proverbs 15:1	
Proverbs 15:23	
Proverbs 17:27	
Proverbs 20:3	

5 DAILY WALK, DAY FIVE

Have you ever stopped to think about when we communicate? It is usually when we are trying to solve a problem: raising children, job dissatisfaction, moving, etc .

Hopefully this study has motivated you and your spouse to communicate in such a way that deepens your intimacy and uplifts your spouse.

If God designed marriage, can He make it work? We found the answer to be a resounding yes.

1. Which of the five faith principles had the biggest impact on your marriage? Why?

_____

_____

_____

2. How have you and your spouse dealt with a struggle or trial differently than you had before this study?

_____

_____

_____

3. Is there anything that has been inhibiting communication in your marriage? It's time to be honest and open up the lines of communication.

_____

_____

4. What have been the most meaningful steps you and your spouse have taken regarding conflict, sexual intimacy, or communication?

_____

_____

_____

Special Note: Please read the week eight notes before meeting as a group.

✦ *Personal Application* ✦

Many of us have something blocking our communication. Like logs in a stream, bitterness, unresolved anger, and resentful feelings jam up honest dialogue. It's time to destroy the dam!

Part One (Personal)

Step One - Pray for clarity and wisdom in how to communicate the issues to your spouse.

Step Two - Write down your negative feelings about past communication.

Step Three - Identify any sinful actions on your part. Be ready to seek forgiveness when you meet as a couple.

Part Two (As a Couple)

Step One - Pray together for authentic communication and grace to resolve the issue.

Step Two - Seek forgiveness for any past selfish or sinful actions in your communication (see 1 John 1:9).

Step Three - Present your negative feelings about past communication.

Step Four - Move towards a biblical resolution of the issue.

Step Five - Commit to each other that you will not allow frustration, bitterness, or unresolved anger to build up in your marriage.

A QUICK LOOK BACK

On the journey from *performance* to *faith* in your marriage, your communication will either stall you out or press you forward. Believers must evaluate their "spirit" when they communicate to their spouse. In addition husbands and wives will need to override their selfish natures with the power of the Spirit if they want to be effective in their communication.

♥2 BECOMING ONE PRAYER
Heavenly Father, I ask You to give me the ability to communicate effectively with You and my spouse. I confess to You that I have not always exhibited the fruit of the Spirit in my communication. Please forgive me. Lord, give me sensitivity to what my human spirit is projecting, especially when I approach my spouse. Give me wisdom from the Scripture to heed its instruction. Give me self-control and gentleness while I encourage and lift up my spouse. By Your grace, allow us to be one in our communication. In the name of Jesus, Amen.

Go ahead and read the Thoughts for the Road and the Continuing the Journey section before your next meeting.

THOUGHTS FOR THE ROAD

Complete the week eight Daily Walks AND read these notes BEFORE coming to your last class.

COMMUNICATION: A KEY TO INTIMACY IN MARRIAGE

So, have you figured out if you operate more like a hand grenade or a land mine in your communication style? Do you lash out in conflict or shrink back?

"We just don't communicate!" How many times have you heard that statement from a frustrated husband or wife? Lack of communication is one of the major causes of divorce in America today.

Tragically, Christian couples do not fare much better than non-Christian couples in the area of communication when they allow their "old natures" to guide their actions instead of the Holy Spirit. Couples who want to become one in marriage must seek God's wisdom concerning communication and resolving conflict. The first step in that direction is for each spouse to have a proper relationship with the Holy Spirit.

Effective communication and conflict resolution skills require couples to embrace the ministry of the Holy Spirit.

Communication is the marital glue of oneness. In week three, we established that the power for oneness comes from the Holy Spirit.

Effective communication is a product of the Holy Spirit.

Communication in marriage can be defined as the truthful and complete sharing of oneself with one's spouse so that both are built up and encouraged toward oneness. The Holy Spirit is vital to this process. In fact, one of the best environments for effective communication is one where the "fruit of the Spirit" is present: "love, joy, peace, patience, kindness, goodness, faithfulness, gentleness and self-control" (Galatians 5:22–23).

The basis of communication is man's living spirit.

The Bible says, "The Lord God formed the man from the dust of the ground and breathed into his nostrils the breath of life, and the man became a living being" (Genesis 2:7). Literally, God breathed "spirit" into man: body plus spirit equals man. God's creation of man's spirit became the basis of all communication—between man and God, as well as between man and man. It was the breathing of spirit into man that set him apart from all other living creatures. This provided a unique way of communication – that of words and emotions.

If a husband and wife are both believers, communication influenced by the Holy Spirit is now possible. God's Spirit energizes their renewed human spirits, and both can better understand Malachi's statement to husbands, "So guard yourself in your spirit, and do not break faith with the wife of your youth" (Malachi 2:15b). Malachi indicates that husbands and wives should take heed to their human spirits.

In 1 Corinthians 2:14, 16, Paul states that believers can understand and apply God's wisdom to their lives: "The man without the Spirit does not accept the things that come from the Spirit of God, for they are foolishness to him, and he cannot understand them, because they are spiritually discerned.... But we have the mind of Christ."

If we have the "mind of Christ," divorce will not be an option. God does not mince words when He speaks on divorce, "For, 'I hate divorce,' says the Lord, the God of Israel" (Malachi 2:16). If we are continually walking in the Spirit, the thought of divorce will not occur. The bottom line to good communication is a commitment to working through problems without

contemplating an end to the marriage relationship.

The question regarding proper communication between you and your spouse then becomes, "Is each of your spirits submitted to the Holy Spirit?" If they are, effective communication is possible.

The Holy Spirit uses Scripture to train couples to be more effective communicators.

When most couples think of communication, their initial thought focuses on the art of speaking. However, Scripture indicates that communication involves the total person, and research verifies this. A classic research study at Stanford University concluded that only 7 percent of our communication occurs from words alone. The tone of one's voice communicates 38 percent, and the other 55 percent involves facial expressions, general posture, as well as body and hand gestures. So, communication involves more than words; it involves the total person, especially the motive of the person's spirit.

Positive aspects of the human spirit benefit communication.

Scripture identifies various positive and negative moods or dispositions that reflect our true spirit. The underlying spirit, which a person projects, will affect his or her communication. Consider these positive moods that reflect one's spirit and will encourage communication. Read each reference:

- A willing spirit—Exodus 35:21; Matthew 26:41
- A fervent spirit—Acts 18:25; Romans 12:11
- A gentle spirit—1 Corinthians 4:21; 5:4; Galatians 6:1
- A unifying spirit—Ephesians 2:22; 4:3; Philippians 1:27; 2:1–2
- A rejoicing spirit—Luke 1:47

Negative aspects of the human spirit hinder communication.

The following negative reflections of man's spirit all hinder communication. Consider each and read the supporting references:

- A wounded spirit—Genesis 26:35; Exodus 6:9; Daniel 2:1
- A sinful or hardened spirit—Numbers 5:14; Deuteronomy 2:30
- An angry spirit—Genesis 4:6–8

We need to ask ourselves, "Am I projecting a positive or negative spirit to my spouse?" and, "Am I allowing the Holy Spirit to influence my human spirit?" As couples sensitively monitor their human spirits and allow the fruit of the Holy Spirit to flow from their lives, good and loving communication will be a natural by-product.

EFFECTIVE COMMUNICATION REQUIRES INTENTIONAL CORRECTIONS.

Countless times, marriage counselors hear frustrated couples cry, "It is impossible—we'll never be able to communicate." When couples reach this degree of discouragement, they can be assured that Satan and sin are involved in the couple's confusion. When sin disrupts our communication, Scripture instructs us to take certain steps to restore the power of the Holy Spirit and to escape Satan's deception.

By a decision of their wills, couples must choose to set aside their old natures and release their new spirits.

Husbands and wives must believe, based on Scripture, that God has truly given them a new capacity available only to believers in Christ. They are "to put off [the] old self, which is being corrupted by its deceitful desires; to renew your minds; and to put on the new self, created to be like God in true righteousness and holiness" (Ephesians 4:22–24).

Encourage each other's spiritual capacity for communication, and motivate each other by complimenting your spouse's efforts.

Couples must put away anger and an unforgiving spirit.

To further ensure peace, Paul wrote: "In your anger do not sin: Do not let the sun go down while you are still angry, and do not give the devil a foothold." The apostle then added:

"Get rid of all bitterness, rage and anger, brawling and slander, along with every form of malice" (Ephesians 4:26–27, 31). When any of these attitudes—anger, bitterness, malice, slander, or rage—are present, edifying communication cannot take place. You and your spouse must realize that these attitudes are the fruit of your old sinful natures.

Unfortunately, these hurtful attitudes are natural. Without aggressive faith, couples will never escape these natural tendencies. It often takes a lot of prayer and, sometimes, wise counsel, to break these habits.

Couples must resolve anger quickly.

Why is it important to resolve conflict quickly, preferably before the sun sets? Because if we don't, things fester and build until they are complicated and insurmountable. Don't go to bed, if at all possible, without resolving your problem. If resolution cannot come before you sleep, set a time the next day to resolve it. The habit of resolving problems quickly encourages an atmosphere of peace and harmony in the home.

Satan wants husbands and wives to focus on the ugliness of their spouse's sins. That way each spouse will naturally feel that his or her own anger and bitterness is reasonable. How many spouses have been devastated by the other saying, "I forgive you, but I will never be able to forget or to trust you again"? Is that really what God meant by forgiving? Certainly not! God forgives and forgets, and desires that we do the same. It may take time, however, to win back the trust.

> The habit of resolving problems quickly encourages an atmosphere of peace and harmony in the home.

Forgiveness if vital for good communication.

The ultimate test of a couple's ability to communicate comes when they attempt to handle conflicts. The following five exhortations, founded on Scripture, are vital to accomplish this successfully.

1. Approach each other with an attitude of kindness and concern (Ephesians 4:29, 32).

Rejection, fear, and bitterness destroy communication, and conflicts cannot be resolved in threatening environments. Therefore, couples must seek God's perspective in establishing an environment of kindness and concern. They are to "be kind and compassionate to one another, forgiving each other, just as in Christ God forgave you" and to "clothe [themselves] with compassion, kindness, humility, gentleness and patience" (Ephesians 4:32; Colossians 3:12).

These attitudes form the "door" to marital communication through which husbands and wives must enter if they hope to resolve their differences.

2. Establish an atmosphere of mutual vulnerability (2 Corinthians 2:4).

Vulnerability is the ability to share one's innermost feelings, thoughts, concerns, and aspirations without fear of rejection. Before differences can be resolved, both spouses must be able to trust each other enough to openly share without being put down or scolded.

Vulnerability requires transparency— showing an honesty and openness in disclosing events, opinions, and feelings.

If one spouse is truly transparent, the other will feel trusted and loved as well as respected. Being vulnerable says, "I respect and trust you enough to be transparent." Transparency says, "I love you" and "I need you."

3. Become effective listeners (James 1:19).

Rather than listening, we usually fall into one of these traps:

- Pretend to hear by not trying to understand.
- Plan your answer before your spouse is done talking.
- Selective hearing – only accept what sounds right to you.
- Come to the conversation with your judgments already made.

4. Effective listening resolves differences by clarifying what the other spouse is really feeling and saying.

Couples who really listen to each other and then act by taking corrective actions will be effective at communicating and resolving conflict. Consider the following five characteristics of effective listening:

- Listening involves creating a non-threatening environment of understanding.
- Listening involves shutting the mouth and paying attention.
- Listening involves seeking clarification.
- Listening involves more than sympathy; it requires empathy.
- Listening involves demonstrating a teachable spirit.

5. Speak the truth in love (Ephesians 4:15).

Here are seven elements to remember when speaking the truth in love.

- The goal should be to restore your spouse (Galatians 6:1).
- The motivation should be to gain understanding (1 Timothy 1:5).
- The method should avoid cutting remarks that could start the "insult cycle" (Proverbs 16:24; 20:3).

More often than not, our tongues block conflict resolution. Criticism and name-calling are destructive. Speaking the truth in love will eliminate reckless tongues. With that in mind, avoid:

- Explosive words
- Sarcasm, ridicule, or innuendo
- Verbal fighting
- Words like "always" and "never"
- Blaming each other

- Your desire should be to keep your emotions under control (Proverbs 14:29).
- A good listening technique is to stop and restate your spouse's argument.
- The timing and setting for your communication is important (Proverbs 15:23; 27:14).
- A prompt resolution is necessary (Ephesians 4:26).

The Bible states that we must be willing to forgive up to 70 times seven (Matthew 18:21-22, NASB). This flows from faith principle four: rather than blame, return a blessing. Giving and receiving forgiveness is a nonnegotiable issue in resolving conflict and creating better communication with your spouse. Your ability to forgive your spouse is directly related to your spouse's ability to rebound from conflict and sin, and also to forgive you.

When you say, "I just can't forgive you for what you did," what you really mean is, "I choose not to forgive you."

Forgiveness is an act of the will based on faith in Christ (see Matthew 6:14–15; Ephesians 4:32).

Why is forgiveness crucial to your marriage communication? Because if unforgiven bitterness and fear fester, the slate is not clear. Couples must be able to forgive for past sins and look to the future with hope. How many times did Christ ask us to forgive? Seventy times seven. When you get to 490, who is counting? Since God graciously has forgiven us, we too must forgive others or we trample the grace God has given us.

When your spouse wrongs you, immediately entrust yourself to the Lord. Seek His perspective on the matter. Leave revenge to the Lord (Romans 12:14–20), knowing that only He can effectively work in your spouse's life. Trust God's promises of future blessings by following His commands.

MOVE QUICKLY TO CONFLICT RESOLUTION.

Once you have confessed negative feelings or behavior to God, it's time to resolve any conflicts with your spouse. Keep in mind that God knows every detail of the conflict. Although there may be a common way of coming to resolution for your problem, He may have a new and creative way of resolving it. Trust Him to lead you to the best method of resolution.

As God leads you and your spouse to resolve conflicts, trust Him that He will also restore positive feelings between yourself and your spouse. If you allow Him, He can completely restore you and your spouse and bring oneness back to your marriage.

To Sum Up…
It is interesting that Peter sums up his chapter on marriage with this statement:

To sum up, let all be harmonious, sympathetic, brotherly, kind-hearted, and humble in spirit, not returning evil for evil, or insult for insult; for you were called for the very purpose that you might inherit a blessing (1 Peter 3:8, NASB).

These characteristics just happen to be the same as those that are attributed to Jesus. If we properly view marriage as God intended, submit to His purposes and plan, walk by the power of the Spirit, learn to love with His love – we truly inherit a blessing. The marriage relationship is a significant tool used to conform us to the image of Christ, and the result is oneness!

Please read on to Continuing the Journey.

Continuing the
JOURNEY

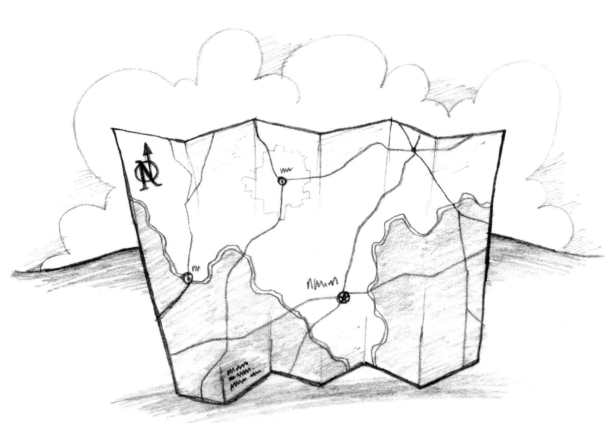

Enjoy life with the woman whom you love

all the days of your fleeting life

which He has given to you under the sun;

for this is your reward in life...

(ECCLESIASTES 9:9).

CONTINUING THE JOURNEY

Hopefully we've come along way in our journey from performance to faith. The lessons learned in this study will only become a reality if we act by faith on the principles God ordained for oneness.

It takes time and effort to fully discover a faith-based relationship. But make no mistake—it starts by understanding and accepting the five faith principles for oneness. From there, when the struggles of marriage come (and remember, they will!), it then becomes our responsibility to act and apply the faith principles.

Marriage, as you know, is more than just a wedding day. It's a journey together. Wouldn't it be great if 1, 5, 10, or 50 years from now, you look back to this study as the first step towards modeling faith in your relationship rather than depending upon performance?

COMMIT TO A LONG-TERM FAITH VISION OF ONENESS IN YOUR MARRIAGE.

A long-term faith vision is vital for lasting oneness in marriage. There are three essential commitments needed for a great marriage. They are: (1) Make your faith commitments, (2) Share your faith commitments with others; and (3) have an ultimate vision to glorify God.

Make the faith commitments in your marriage now.

The distinctive trait of a faith relationship is that both spouses look beyond each other's performance to God's sovereignty and promises. As you review the five faith principles, draw a line in the sand with your marriage. Make a commitment today to weave these principles into your daily life.

FAITH PRINCIPLE NUMBER ONE:

By faith, we must commit ourselves to God's purposes of reflecting His image, reproducing a godly heritage, and reigning in spiritual warfare.

FAITH PRINCIPLE NUMBER TWO:

By faith, we must receive our spouse from God as His personal provision for our individual needs.

FAITH PRINCIPLE NUMBER THREE:

By faith, we must daily commit to release the power of the Holy Spirit in our lives.

FAITH PRINCIPLE NUMBER FOUR:

By faith, we must submit to the only active and reactive biblical forces for change in marriage: agape love and blessing.

FAITH PRINCIPLE NUMBER FIVE:

By faith, we must seek God's wisdom concerning our responsibilities of mutual love and respect.

Only when you and your spouse understand and individually commit to the above faith beliefs will you as a couple be able to journey to a *faith-based relationship.*

FINISH THE JOURNEY BY SHARING AND GLORIFYING GOD.

*R*emember, to the extent a relationship is not of faith, it is based on performance, which leads ultimately to disappointment, hurt, rejection, and bitterness.

Faith, on the other hand, leads to hope, compassion, creativity, and *agape* love. You and your spouse are either living by faith or by performance.

Keep these faith commitments vital in your lives by sharing them with others.

Many couples hear these faith principles and commit only halfheartedly to them. Then, after a short time, they lose touch with the principles and begin to doubt their commitments. Sharing these faith principles with others is an invaluable way to keep your faith commitment vital in your marriage. Two things happen when you take responsibility for sharing biblical truths with others. First, you are reminded and renewed in your own marriage. Second, when you dare to share with others, your understanding deepens because you must answer the questions of others.

Paul was aware of these benefits when he instructed Timothy, "And the things you have heard me say in the presence of many witnesses entrust to reliable [people] who will also be qualified to teach others" (2 Timothy 2:2).

This small group study was written with the intent of helping you enter this process. If you noticed, the couples leading this study were not required to be "teachers." Almost anyone who enjoys people can learn to lead a group. Ask your leader how you can become part of helping couples follow these principles of oneness by facilitating another class.

2 Timothy 2:2 tells us to teach others. Why? Because it's as we teach others, the principles go so much deeper into our own lives. If this study has impacted your life, we would encourage and challenge you to become facilitators of marriage classes. As you help others, you will be surprised at how much your marriage will deepen.

> Sharing these faith principles with others is an invaluable way to keep your faith commitment vital in your marriage.

Have a vision beyond your marriage: to glorify God.

God wants couples to become one in their marriages so that they might be equipped to effectively serve and glorify Him. This commission fits well with the marital commission in Genesis 1 to reflect God's image, reproduce His image through a godly heritage, and reign over the earth through spiritual warfare.

As we serve the Lord, our marriages greatly benefit. They become more purposeful and productive. They face less pressure, as each spouse's gifts and talents become more important.

In addition, when we make *serving and glorifying God our primary marriage goal*, it will never become outdated. If you live to be eighty, serving God will never grow stale. Your children may leave home and you might retire from your vocation, but your joy in serving God will never fade. Ministry grows better with age. It assures purpose and productivity in your marriage and your life until the Lord calls you home. And no matter what your age, race, or economic situation, you and your spouse will thrive in service to the King. John Piper in his book *Desiring God*, got it right when he said, "God is most glorified in us when we are most satisfied in Him." The continuing journey finds its most basic satisfaction in God alone, not in our marriages, our mates, or our children. He alone is the Author and Perfector of our ongoing marital journey. The triune of God alone is the means of the ongoing journey as well as its goal.

God is faithful to His Word. If you

will learn and make these faith commitments and then constantly renew your understanding of them by teaching others, you will experience God's blessings for a lifetime together.

Enjoy life with the woman whom you love all the days of your fleeting life which he has give to you under the sun; for this is your reward in life..... (ECCLESIASTES 9:9).

And finally, one closing thought. The journey into marital joy and intimacy will never find its ultimate fulfillment here in this world and in this life, no matter how great our motives or principles. It is as C.S. Lewis has rightly said in his book *Mere Christianity*, there is a new world coming in which our ultimate longings will finally come true:

> The journey into marital joy and intimacy will never find its ultimate fulfillment here in this world and in this life.

The Christian says, "Creatures are not born with desires unless satisfaction for those desires exists. A baby feels hunger: well, there is such a thing as food. A duckling wants to swim: well, there is such a thing as water. Men feel sexual desire: well, there is such a thing as sex. If I find myself a desire which no experience in this world can satisfy, the most probable explanation is that I was made for another world. If none of my earthly pleasures satisfy it, that does not prove that the universe is fraud. Probably earthly treasures were never meant to satisfy it, but only to arouse it, to suggest the real thing. If that is so, I must take care, on the one hand, never to despise, or be unthankful for, these earthly blessings, and on the other, never to mistake them for the something else of which they are only a kind of copy, or echo, or mirage. I must keep alive in myself the desire for my true country, which I shall not find till after death; I must make it the main object of life to press on to that other country and to help others to do the same." (C. S. Lewis)

Heavenly Father, thank You for the way Your Word has transformed my perspective of marriage over these past eight weeks. By Your grace, Lord, I pray that You would build a spiritual wall around us so that nothing can rob us of our oneness. I pray, Lord, that we would realize what a spiritual war we are in. Lord, I personally commit to be involved in helping teach others these truths in the future. I look forward to training my children. I pray that our marriage would accomplish Your will of reflecting Your image, reproducing a godly heritage, and reigning in spiritual warfare all the days of our lives. In the name of Jesus, Amen.

Christian Family Life wishes you God's best in building your *faith relationship*. Thank you for taking the time to be a part of this study. We hope you have been challenged and rewarded. We also thank the leaders of this class for committing to share these truths with you. We pray that you, too, will become leaders, taking others through this life-changing material on marriage. May God richly bless your lives as you seek to follow Him.

MEET THE CREATORS OF THE JOURNEY

The Two Becoming One small group study has been developed by the Christian Family Life ministry. The vision of Christian Family Life is "Teaching Christians God's faith principles for relationships so that they may know Christ more intimately and be freed to serve Him more effectively." That is the goal of this workbook and your group study.

Christian Family Life was founded in 1971 as several couples from various church backgrounds joined Don and Sally Meredith in their pursuit of biblical principles of marriage. These included Dr. Barry and Mary Leventhal and Dr. Joseph and Linda Dillow among others. They began searching the Scriptures, and from their study of Genesis 1 and 2 and Ephesians 5, the supernatural faith principles discussed in this workbook began to surface. Don and Sally also co-founded the Family Life Ministry of Campus Crusade for Christ. Many of the faith principles taught in this study are presented in the popular "Weekend

to Remember" seminars presented by the Family Life ministry.

Several talented couples and individuals have been indispensable to the development and publication of this workbook. Dr. Barry Leventhal has continued to influence this material from it's inception through the many forms it has taken for over thirty years. We are indebted to a gifted writer, Brian Goins, for his incredible "way with words" throughout this manual. We appreciate Chuck and Lorianne Merritt for their encouragement, invaluable input and publishing ability for over a decade.

Since its inception in 1971, Christian Family Life has presented the principles found in this study to hundreds of thousands of people (through seminars and classes). If you would like more information about these principles or being a group study leader, feel free to contact us at:

Christian Family Life, Inc.
(800) 264-3876
or by visiting our website at:
www.2becoming1.com

PRAYER JOURNAL

"Pray for one another" (JAMES 5:16 NASB).

Name_____   Spouse _____

Home Phone _____   Children (ages)_____

Business Phone _____   _____

Home Address _____   _____

_____   _____

Week	Prayer Request(s)	Answers to Prayer
1		
2		
3		
4		
5		
6		
7		
8	My long-term prayer request(s):	

PRAYER JOURNAL

"Pray for one another" (JAMES 5:16 NASB).

Name_____   Spouse _____

Home Phone _____   Children (ages)_____

Business Phone _____   _____

Home Address _____   _____

_____   _____

Week	Prayer Request(s)	Answers to Prayer
1		
2		
3		
4		
5		
6		
7		
8	My long-term prayer request(s):	

PRAYER JOURNAL

"Pray for one another" (JAMES 5:16 NASB).

Name_____   Spouse _____

Home Phone _____   Children (ages) _____

Business Phone _____   _____

Home Address _____   _____

_____   _____

Week	Prayer Request(s)	Answers to Prayer
1		
2		
3		
4		
5		
6		
7		
8	My long-term prayer request(s):	

PRAYER JOURNAL

"Pray for one another" (JAMES 5:16 NASB).

Name_____   Spouse _____

Home Phone _____   Children (ages)_____

Business Phone _____   _____

Home Address _____   _____

_____   _____

Week	Prayer Request(s)	Answers to Prayer
1		
2		
3		
4		
5		
6		
7		
8	My long-term prayer request(s):	

PRAYER JOURNAL

"Pray for one another" (JAMES 5:16 NASB).

Name_____   Spouse _____

Home Phone _____   Children (ages)_____

Business Phone _____   _____

Home Address _____   _____

_____   _____

Week	Prayer Request(s)	Answers to Prayer
1		
2		
3		
4		
5		
6		
7		
8	My long-term prayer request(s):	

PRAYER JOURNAL

"Pray for one another" (JAMES 5:16 NASB).

Name_____   Spouse _____

Home Phone _____   Children (ages)_____

Business Phone _____   _____

Home Address _____   _____

_____   _____

Week	Prayer Request(s)	Answers to Prayer
1		
2		
3		
4		
5		
6		
7		
8	My long-term prayer request(s):	

PRAYER JOURNAL

"Pray for one another" (JAMES 5:16 NASB).

Name_____   Spouse _____

Home Phone _____   Children (ages) _____

Business Phone _____   _____

Home Address _____   _____

_____   _____

Week	Prayer Request(s)	Answers to Prayer
1		
2		
3		
4		
5		
6		
7		
8	My long-term prayer request(s):	

RECOMMITMENT OF MARRIAGE VOWS

[Each couple should hold hands while the leader reads aloud the following passage:]

"Will you accept your spouse as a gift from God and pledge to keep him or her in all love and honor, in all duty and service, in all faith and tenderness, to live with and cherish according to the ordinance of God, in the holy bond of marriage, including the following commitments? If so, say 'We do' after each of the following statements.

- Do you commit to base your relationship on faith rather than performance?
- Do you commit to accomplish God's purpose for your marriage by reflecting God's image, reproducing a godly heritage, and reigning in spiritual warfare together?
- Do you commit to receive your spouse as God's personal provision for your aloneness needs?
- Do you commit to allow God's Holy Spirit to control all aspects of your marriage?
- Do you commit to love (agape) your spouse sacrificially?
- Do you commit to return a blessing when wronged?
- Do you commit to trust God's wisdom in your roles of love and submission?
- Do you commit to follow God's principles of communication?
- Do you commit to follow God's principles of resolving conflicts?
- Do you commit to aggressively seek God's perspective on sex and romance?
- Do you commit to recognize and seek God's perspective concerning trials?

"If you, as a couple united in oneness, have answered 'We do' to each of the above commitments, then, as individual couples, read aloud the following statement to each other."

[Each husband reads the following statement of marriage recommitment to his wife. After the husband has recited his recommitment, his wife responds by reading her recommitment to the husband.]

"Today, before God Almighty, and in full appreciation of God's biblical purposes for marriage,

I, _____, recommit to you, _____, to be my wedded husband/wife. I promise and covenant before God and these witnesses to be your loving and faithful husband/wife in plenty and in want, in joy and in sorrow, in sickness and in health, as long as we both shall live. In the name of the Father, and of the Son, and of the Holy Spirit. Amen."

We sign our names in witness to the above recommitment, as an indication of our desire to honor each other and glorify God through the power of the Holy Spirit.

Signed:

Husband _____ Witnesses _____

Wife _____ _____

Date: _____/_____/_____

MEMORY VERSE CARDS

WEEK ONE MEMORY VERSE:
*God created man in His own image,
in the image of God He created him;
male and female He created them*
(GENESIS 1:27).

WEEK FIVE MEMORY VERSE:
*Submit to one another
out of reverence for Christ*
(EPHESIANS 5:21).

WEEK TWO MEMORY VERSE:
*For this cause a man shall leave
his father and his mother,
and shall cleave to his wife;
and they shall become one flesh*
(GENESIS 2:24, NASB).

WEEK SIX MEMORY VERSE:
*Consider it all joy, my brethren, when you
encounter various trials, knowing that the testing
of your faith produces endurance, and let
endurance have its perfect result, that you may
be perfect and complete, lacking in nothing*
(JAMES 1:2-4, NASB).

WEEK THREE MEMORY VERSE:
*But the Helper, the Holy Spirit,
whom the Father will send in My name,
He will teach you all things,
and bring to your remembrance
all that I said to you*
(JOHN 14:26, NASB).

WEEK SEVEN MEMORY VERSE (WIVES):
*My beloved is mine, and I am his...his desire
is for me* (SONG OF SOLOMON 2:16; 7:10, NASB).

WEEK SEVEN MEMORY VERSE (HUSBANDS):
*Rejoice in the wife of your youth...
may you ever be captivated by her love*
(PROVERBS 5:18-19).

WEEK FOUR MEMORY VERSE
*Do nothing out of selfish ambition
or vain conceit, but in humility consider others
better than yourselves. Each of you should
look not only to your own interests,
but also to the interests of others*
(PHILIPPIANS 2:3–4).

WEEK EIGHT MEMORY VERSE:
*Do not let any unwholesome talk
come out of your mouths, but only what is helpful
for building others up according to their needs,
that it may benefit those who listen*
(EPHESIANS 4:29).